AI-POWERED STRATEGIES

Interdisciplinary Insights for Global Finance, Economics, and Strategic Business Management

CONSULTORIA IA

Copyright © 2024 CONSULTORIA IA

All rights reserved

The characters and events portrayed in this book are fictitious. Any similarity to real persons, living or dead, is coincidental and not intended by the author.

No part of this book may be reproduced, or stored in a retrieval system, or transmitted in any form or by any means, electronic, mechanical, photocopying, recording, or otherwise, without express written permission of the publisher.

Cover design by: Art Painter
Library of Congress Control Number: 2018675309
Printed in the United States of America

TO OUR FAMILY

CONTENTS

Title Page

Copyright

Dedication

Brief Review

Why Read This Book?

Target Audience

Preface

Chapter 1: The AI Revolution in Finance – Transforming Markets and Modeling Risk

Chapter 2: Economic Forecasting Redefined – Harnessing AI for Precision and Speed

Chapter 3: Strategic Business Management – Leveraging AI for Competitive Edge

Chapter 4: Navigating Ethical AI – Responsible Implementation in Global Business

Chapter 5: The Future is Now – Integrating AI into Long-Term Strategic Planning

Appendices

BRIEF REVIEW

AI-Powered Strategies: Interdisciplinary Insights for Global Finance, Economics, and Strategic Business Management is an eBook that delves into how artificial intelligence (AI) is reshaping the fields of global finance, economics, and strategic business management. As the author, I provide an in-depth exploration of the convergence of these disciplines, illustrating how AI tools are revolutionizing decision-making, optimizing processes, and driving innovation in a complex and competitive global landscape.

The book covers practical case studies, emerging theories, and strategic frameworks, equipping professionals, academics, and business leaders with the knowledge to harness AI effectively and ethically. From risk modeling in finance to using algorithms for forecasting economic trends and enhancing operational efficiency, this resource offers a comprehensive and multidimensional approach to navigating the intersection of technology and business.

WHY READ THIS BOOK?

AI-Powered Strategies: Interdisciplinary Insights for Global Finance, Economics, and Strategic Business Management is essential reading for anyone looking to stay ahead in an era where AI technology is redefining business landscapes. Here's why this book stands out:

1. Comprehensive Understanding: It bridges finance, economics, and strategic management, providing a holistic view of how AI is influencing these interconnected fields.

2. Practical Applications: The book goes beyond theory, showcasing real-world case studies and actionable strategies that can be implemented in various business contexts.

3. Cutting-Edge Insights: Stay informed with the latest trends and innovations in AI, gaining an edge in decision-making and strategic planning.

4. Ethical and Effective Use: It emphasizes responsible AI implementation, balancing technological advancements with ethical considerations to create sustainable practices.

5. Expert Guidance: Whether you're a business leader, financial analyst, or student, this book equips you with tools and knowledge to leverage AI confidently and competently.

This book is an indispensable guide for navigating the complexities of the modern business world powered by AI.

TARGET AUDIENCE

AI-Powered Strategies: Interdisciplinary Insights for Global Finance, Economics, and Strategic Business Management is tailored for a diverse audience that spans across several fields and professional levels. The key target groups include:

1. Business Leaders and Executives: CEOs, CFOs, and decision-makers looking to integrate AI solutions into their strategic planning and operational processes.

2. Financial Professionals: Analysts, investment managers, and risk officers who want to harness AI for improved data analysis, forecasting, and portfolio management.

3. Economists and Policy Makers: Individuals focused on understanding how AI impacts economic models, market behavior, and regulatory frameworks.

4. Academics and Researchers: Scholars in finance, economics, business management, and computer science who are exploring interdisciplinary applications of AI.

5. Entrepreneurs and Innovators: Startups and tech-driven businesses interested in leveraging AI for competitive advantage and business growth.

6. Students and Educators: Business, finance, and technology students aiming to deepen their understanding of AI applications in a global context, along with instructors seeking comprehensive resources for curriculum development.

7. Consultants and Strategic Advisors: Professionals providing guidance to clients in industries looking to adopt AI for strategic improvements.

PREFACE

In a rapidly evolving world where technology continues to transform the way we live and work, artificial intelligence (AI) has emerged as a pivotal force reshaping industries, economies, and strategic business practices. The impetus for writing AI-Powered Strategies: Interdisciplinary Insights for Global Finance, Economics, and Strategic Business Management was born out of a recognition that we are not just witnessing incremental changes, but a profound shift that demands a deep and nuanced understanding across multiple disciplines.

This book was crafted for leaders, professionals, academics, and students who are navigating this complex landscape and seeking to leverage AI in ways that drive innovation, efficiency, and sustainable growth. The intersections of finance, economics, and strategic business management offer fertile ground for exploring how AI can solve complex problems, inform better decision-making, and anticipate future challenges.

Throughout the pages of this book, readers will find an interdisciplinary approach that combines practical insights, theoretical perspectives, and case studies from real-world applications. It is designed to provide both a comprehensive overview and targeted strategies that readers can adapt to their specific contexts. As much as this is a guide to understanding AI's potential, it is also a call to consider the ethical implications and challenges that come with adopting such powerful technologies.

I invite you to explore this journey where technology meets strategy, where data meets decision-making, and where innovation meets responsibility. My hope is that this book empowers you with knowledge, sparks curiosity, and equips you with the tools to make informed, strategic, and forward-thinking choices in an AI-driven world.

CHAPTER 1: THE AI REVOLUTION IN FINANCE – TRANSFORMING MARKETS AND MODELING RISK

The world of finance is undergoing a seismic transformation, driven by the inexorable rise of artificial intelligence (AI). From trading floors to regulatory frameworks, the influence of AI is not just palpable; it is revolutionary, redefining every dimension of how markets operate and how financial risk is modeled. To grasp the full impact of AI on global finance, one must first recognize that we are living in a period reminiscent of the industrial revolution—only this time, it is algorithms, not steam engines, driving profound change.

The Evolution of AI in Finance

The integration of AI into finance did not occur overnight. Decades of academic research and technological advancements have laid the groundwork for this transformation. Early forms of algorithmic trading, pioneered in the late 20th century, relied heavily on rule-based systems that executed trades based on pre-programmed instructions. Although these systems provided the market with higher levels of efficiency and speed, they lacked the ability to learn and adapt dynamically to changing conditions. It is the advent of machine learning (ML) and deep learning technologies that has catalyzed a new era, one where computers are not just passive executors but active learners and predictors.

AI technologies in finance can be broadly categorized into three essential areas: predictive analytics, natural language processing (NLP), and reinforcement learning. Predictive analytics has revolutionized the way financial institutions forecast market movements. Machine learning models now analyze massive troves of data—ranging from historical prices and economic indicators to real-time social media sentiment—enabling traders and analysts to anticipate market trends with unprecedented accuracy. Meanwhile, NLP tools have become indispensable for processing the enormous volume of unstructured data generated daily, such as news articles, regulatory filings, and financial reports. These AI-driven systems extract meaningful insights from the flood of information, allowing investors to make informed decisions more efficiently than ever before. Finally, reinforcement learning, inspired by behavioral psychology, has entered the fray. In this paradigm, AI algorithms are trained to optimize complex strategies through trial and error, much like a human learning from experience.

How AI Transforms Financial Markets

One of the most striking manifestations of AI in finance is its impact on financial markets, particularly in the realm of trading and market efficiency. High-frequency trading (HFT) firms, such as Renaissance Technologies and Citadel, are emblematic of how AI-driven strategies have come to dominate market activities. These firms deploy complex, data-intensive algorithms to execute thousands of trades in milliseconds, capitalizing on minuscule price discrepancies and arbitrage opportunities. Speed is of the essence, and AI systems have made human intervention virtually obsolete in this domain. The outcome? An environment where liquidity is abundant but where volatility can also be amplified by algorithms reacting to similar signals en masse. The "flash crash" of May 6, 2010, serves as a cautionary tale of how quickly automated systems can unravel market stability, underscoring the need for robust risk management mechanisms.

Beyond HFT, AI's role in asset management has seen remarkable progress. Traditional investment strategies, driven by fundamental analysis or quantitative models, are being augmented or even supplanted by AI-driven approaches. Hedge funds and asset management firms increasingly employ AI to identify patterns that human analysts may overlook. These patterns are not confined to the usual suspects like stock prices or interest rates but extend to obscure correlations hidden deep within alternative data sets—such as satellite imagery of parking lots to predict retail performance or tracking the shipping routes of oil tankers to forecast commodity prices. The sheer volume and diversity of data that AI can analyze has granted investors a competitive edge in discovering alpha—investment returns that surpass the market average.

Modeling Risk in the Age of AI

If AI's capacity to enhance trading and investment strategies is awe-inspiring, its implications for risk management are equally transformative. One of the most persistent challenges in finance has been accurately modeling risk, particularly in a world characterized by black swan events—rare, unforeseen occurrences with severe consequences. The 2008 global financial crisis is a poignant example of the limitations of traditional risk models, which failed to anticipate the cascading effects of a subprime mortgage meltdown. AI offers a potential antidote to this problem, promising not only more robust risk assessments but also the ability to adapt to new forms of systemic risk.

Machine learning models in risk management excel in identifying non-linear relationships and uncovering latent risk factors that would elude classical econometric models. Credit risk assessment, for instance, has been revolutionized by AI, particularly in emerging markets where traditional credit scoring systems are inadequate. By analyzing an eclectic mix of data points—ranging from mobile phone usage patterns to social media activity—AI models can generate more comprehensive and fair risk profiles for individuals and corporations alike. This democratization of credit access is particularly transformative for underbanked populations, facilitating financial inclusion on an unprecedented scale.

It is not just credit risk that AI is reshaping. Market risk and operational risk are also benefiting from AI-enhanced modeling. Take the case of value-at-risk (VaR), a staple metric used to estimate the potential loss in the value of a portfolio under normal market conditions. Traditional VaR models are based on assumptions that may not hold during periods of market stress. AI introduces a more adaptive approach, using techniques such as deep learning to simulate thousands of market scenarios and stress-test portfolios under diverse conditions. The result is a more resilient framework for navigating uncertainty, though critics rightly point out that these models are still susceptible to the same limitations that plague all risk assessments: the inability to predict the unpredictable.

AI is revolutionizing operational risk management by automating compliance and fraud detection processes. Natural language processing algorithms can monitor communications within financial institutions to detect insider trading or market manipulation. Similarly, machine learning models are adept at identifying suspicious transaction patterns, providing an additional layer of security for banking institutions. The integration of AI in these domains not only enhances the effectiveness of risk management but also introduces efficiencies that reduce operational costs.

The Ethical and Regulatory Quagmire

While the benefits of AI in finance are immense, the rise of AI also raises significant ethical and regulatory questions. The opaque nature of some AI models—often described as "black boxes"—presents a dilemma for both practitioners and regulators. How can one trust a risk assessment or trading algorithm whose inner workings are too complex for even its developers to fully understand? This lack of transparency is not merely a philosophical concern; it has real-world implications for market stability and regulatory compliance.

Regulators around the world are grappling with how to strike the right balance between fostering innovation and ensuring that AI does not exacerbate systemic risk. The European Union's General Data Protection Regulation (GDPR) and its proposed AI Act represent attempts to impose a framework for accountability, yet such regulations are often at odds with the fast pace of technological advancement. In the United States, the Securities and Exchange Commission (SEC) has also begun scrutinizing the use of AI in finance, especially regarding potential biases in credit scoring and investment algorithms. The question remains: how can regulations keep up with technologies that evolve in real-time?

Ethical dilemmas further complicate the landscape. Bias in AI models is a growing concern, particularly in credit and hiring decisions. Even the most advanced algorithms are only as unbiased as the data they are trained on, and historical biases can perpetuate inequities if not carefully addressed. Moreover, the concentration of AI technology within a handful of powerful institutions could exacerbate wealth disparities, as those with access to superior AI models capture a disproportionate share of financial gains.

The Future: A Co-Evolutionary Path Forward

As we look to the future, it is clear that the relationship between AI and finance will be one of co-evolution. Financial institutions must continually adapt to the capabilities of AI, while AI technology will, in turn, shape the evolution of global finance. What might this future look like? One possibility is the increased personalization of financial services, where AI-driven robo-advisors craft bespoke investment strategies based on individual risk tolerances, life goals, and even psychological profiles. Another potential development is the further democratization of financial markets, facilitated by decentralized finance (DeFi) platforms that leverage AI to offer sophisticated financial products without traditional intermediaries.

The intersection of AI and environmental, social, and governance (ESG) criteria also holds promise. AI's ability to analyze environmental impact and social responsibility data could transform how investors allocate capital, promoting more sustainable business practices. Yet, the ultimate impact of AI in finance will depend on how well humanity addresses the twin challenges of ethical governance and robust regulation. Financial markets are, after all, a human construct, and their purpose should be to serve the broader economy and society.

As we stand on the brink of this AI-driven transformation, one thing is certain: the revolution in finance is only just beginning. We are entering an era where algorithms wield immense power, yet the human ability to provide oversight, judgment, and ethical guidance will remain crucial. In this complex dance between man and machine, the hope is that AI will not just be a tool for profit but a force for good—reshaping markets in ways that are fair, efficient, and resilient to the risks of tomorrow.

The AI Revolution in Finance: Navigating Controversies

Despite the immense potential and tangible benefits that artificial intelligence has already brought to the world of finance, its integration is fraught with controversy. These disputes stem from three major areas of concern: transparency and explainability, ethical biases and fairness, and systemic risk and market stability. Each of these issues poses significant questions about the limits of technology and the responsibilities of those who wield it. As we navigate this landscape, it is essential to explore the real-world implications of these controversies and understand how they shape the future of finance.

Controversy 1: Transparency and Explainability – The "Black Box" Problem

One of the most pervasive criticisms of AI in finance is its lack of transparency, often referred to as the "black box" problem. At the heart of this issue lies the difficulty in understanding how and why certain AI models make the decisions they do. Unlike traditional financial models, which are generally grounded in well-established mathematical principles and economic theories, many AI algorithms—especially those employing deep learning—operate in ways that are opaque, even to their developers. This opacity raises significant concerns, particularly in high-stakes scenarios such as loan approvals, trading decisions, and risk assessments.

Consider, for instance, the case of credit scoring. Financial institutions increasingly rely on machine learning models to assess the creditworthiness of individuals. These models are trained on vast datasets, which may include information as varied as an applicant's social media activity, spending habits, and even the words they use in email communications. While this approach has the advantage of harnessing a multitude of signals to make more accurate predictions, it can lead to situations where a loan application is rejected without a clear explanation. If an applicant inquires why they were denied credit, the response may be as unsatisfactory as "the algorithm determined it was too risky," with no insight into the specific factors involved. For consumers, this lack of clarity undermines trust in the financial system and raises issues of accountability.

The implications extend to trading algorithms as well. Imagine a deep learning model deployed by a hedge fund that autonomously executes trades based on patterns it has learned from historical market data. If the algorithm triggers an unexpected cascade of trades that destabilizes the market or results in significant losses, who is held responsible? The fund managers may struggle to explain the model's actions, given that even they cannot fully interpret the internal workings of the AI. This scenario highlights the regulatory conundrum: How can financial regulators ensure oversight and prevent malfeasance when the logic behind decisions is effectively inaccessible?

Attempts to address the transparency issue have led to a burgeoning field known as "explainable AI" (XAI). Researchers and practitioners are working to develop models that are not only powerful but also interpretable. Some financial institutions are experimenting with hybrid models that combine traditional econometric approaches with AI, aiming to maintain a degree of explainability while still leveraging the predictive power of machine learning. Yet, progress is slow, and for now, the balance between performance and transparency remains precarious.

Controversy 2: Ethical Biases and Fairness – The Hidden Prejudices of AI

AI models are only as unbiased as the data they are trained on, and this truth has given rise to a second major controversy: the issue of ethical biases. When financial institutions deploy AI systems, they may inadvertently perpetuate or even amplify societal biases embedded in historical data. This problem is particularly acute in areas such as credit scoring, hiring practices, and fraud detection, where algorithmic decisions can significantly impact people's lives and livelihoods.

One high-profile example of this controversy emerged with a 2019 report involving Apple's credit card, issued in partnership with Goldman Sachs. Numerous users complained that the AI-based credit limit algorithm discriminated against women, granting them lower credit limits compared to men with similar financial profiles. In one particularly well-publicized case, tech entrepreneur David Heinemeier Hansson tweeted that he received a credit limit 20 times higher than his wife, despite her having a better credit score. The backlash was swift, prompting a regulatory inquiry by the New York Department of Financial Services. While Goldman Sachs denied any wrongdoing, the incident underscored the potential for AI to reinforce gender disparities inadvertently.

Similar concerns have been raised about racial bias in AI models. Research has shown that predictive policing algorithms, which are sometimes adopted by financial institutions to assess the risk of loan defaults in high-crime areas, may disproportionately penalize minority communities. These algorithms are trained on historical crime data, which itself may reflect systemic inequalities, such as over-policing of certain neighborhoods. The result is a feedback loop where marginalized groups face higher barriers to financial access, perpetuating cycles of disadvantage.

The financial sector is not blind to these issues, and several initiatives aim to promote fairness in AI. One approach is to ensure that datasets are representative and free from historical biases as much as possible. Another is to implement fairness-aware algorithms that are designed to minimize disparate impacts across demographic groups. Yet, even these efforts face limitations. Bias is a deeply ingrained societal issue, and merely adjusting algorithms cannot fully eliminate its effects. Moreover, trade-offs often emerge: improving fairness in one area may lead to reduced accuracy in another, complicating the decision-making process for financial institutions.

The ethical dilemmas posed by AI have spurred calls for more robust regulation and oversight. Consumer advocacy groups argue that financial institutions should be legally required to audit their AI systems for fairness, much like how public companies are audited for financial transparency. However, some industry leaders warn that overly stringent regulations could stifle innovation. The debate over how to balance fairness with efficiency is far from resolved, and it remains one of the thorniest challenges facing the financial sector.

Controversy 3: Systemic Risk and Market Stability – The Double-Edged Sword of Automation

The third major controversy centers on the systemic risks that AI could introduce to financial markets. While automation promises greater efficiency and the ability to manage risk more effectively, it also poses new dangers that are not yet fully understood. The complexity and interconnectedness of AI systems make it difficult to predict how they will behave in times of market stress, and this uncertainty is a source of growing concern.

A prime example of this risk was the "flash crash" of May 6, 2010, a sudden and severe drop in U.S. equity markets that occurred within minutes, wiping out nearly $1 trillion in market value before recovering just as quickly. Although high-frequency trading algorithms were not the sole cause, they played a significant role in exacerbating the crisis. As sell orders cascaded, algorithms responded by executing trades at lightning speed, creating a feedback loop that intensified the volatility. The flash crash was a stark warning about the potential for automated systems to destabilize markets, particularly when they act in concert.

More recently, in March 2020, during the onset of the COVID-19 pandemic, financial markets experienced unprecedented levels of volatility. While some AI-driven trading strategies performed admirably, others failed spectacularly, highlighting the limitations of algorithms trained on historical data. These models were not designed to handle a global pandemic, a black swan event that defied conventional market dynamics. The turmoil raised questions about the resilience of AI systems and whether they could exacerbate market downturns in future crises.

Systemic risk is not limited to trading algorithms. AI models used in credit markets could also contribute to instability. Imagine a scenario where machine learning models across multiple banks simultaneously adjust their credit risk assessments based on new economic data. If these models all decide to tighten lending standards at the same time, it could trigger a credit crunch, exacerbating an economic downturn. The synchronization of AI-driven decisions, coupled with the speed at which they are executed, introduces new vulnerabilities that traditional risk management frameworks are ill-equipped to handle.

Financial regulators are increasingly aware of these dangers, and some have begun to implement measures to mitigate systemic risk. The Bank of England and the European Central Bank, for example, have called for stress tests specifically designed for AI-driven financial systems. These stress tests aim to simulate extreme scenarios and evaluate how algorithms would behave under such conditions. However, given the rapid pace of AI development, regulatory oversight often lags behind technological advancements, leaving markets exposed to unforeseen risks.

Balancing Innovation and Stability: The Path Forward

The controversies surrounding AI in finance highlight a fundamental tension between innovation and stability. On the one hand, AI offers remarkable opportunities to make financial markets more efficient, inclusive, and adaptive. On the other hand, its potential downsides—ranging from opaque decision-making and ethical biases to systemic risk—cannot be ignored. The path forward will require a collaborative effort among technologists, financial institutions, regulators, and ethicists to ensure that AI serves the greater good.

One promising development is the establishment of industry-wide standards for ethical AI. Organizations such as the Partnership on AI and the Global AI Ethics Consortium are working to create guidelines that promote transparency, fairness, and accountability. These initiatives encourage financial institutions to adopt best practices, such as using interpretable models for high-impact decisions and auditing algorithms for bias regularly.

Advancements in AI governance are likely to play a critical role. Explainable AI techniques are becoming more sophisticated, offering hope that even complex models can be made more transparent. In the future, we may see a greater emphasis on "human-in-the-loop" systems, where human oversight is embedded into automated processes to mitigate risks. For instance, trading algorithms could be programmed to seek human approval before executing trades during periods of extreme market volatility.

The question of regulation remains contentious. While some argue that self-regulation by the industry is sufficient, others advocate for a more proactive regulatory approach. Policymakers face the daunting task of crafting rules that do not stifle innovation but still protect the financial system from AI-induced shocks. This balance will be crucial in determining whether AI fulfills its promise as a transformative force for good or becomes a source of new and unpredictable crises.

The AI revolution in finance is as complex as it is transformative. The technology has already reshaped markets and risk management in profound ways, yet it also brings to light significant ethical, regulatory, and systemic challenges. How these controversies are addressed will define the future of finance, influencing not only who prospers but also how stable and equitable the global financial system remains. As we navigate this uncharted territory, it is clear that the debate over AI in finance is just beginning—and the stakes could not be higher.

CHAPTER 2: ECONOMIC FORECASTING REDEFINED – HARNESSING AI FOR PRECISION AND SPEED

In today's rapidly evolving economic landscape, precision and speed have become indispensable. Traditional economic forecasting models, though useful in a bygone era, struggle to keep pace with the multifaceted and hyper-connected dynamics of the global economy. From currency fluctuations to global supply chain disruptions, the ability to make accurate predictions is paramount, but also more challenging than ever. Enter Artificial Intelligence (AI) – a transformative force poised to revolutionize the very fabric of economic forecasting. By leveraging machine learning, neural networks, and data-driven algorithms, AI is redefining how we anticipate market trends, policy impacts, and financial shifts. In this chapter, we explore how AI is harnessed for unparalleled precision and speed in economic forecasting, drawing on concrete examples and examining the strategic advantages for businesses, investors, and policymakers.

The Shortcomings of Traditional Forecasting Models

Traditional economic forecasting has relied heavily on econometric models, which are mathematical constructs that assume linear relationships between a set of economic variables. These models, like the Keynesian and Classical frameworks, function based on predefined equations where economic growth, inflation, or unemployment rates are expected to move in predictable patterns. However, real-world economies do not operate in linear simplicity. They are subject to shocks and unpredictable events, such as the global financial crisis of 2008 or the unprecedented disruptions caused by the COVID-19 pandemic. Econometric models, with their static assumptions and rigid structures, often fail to capture these nonlinear dynamics, leading to inaccurate or delayed forecasts.

One fundamental issue with traditional models is their reliance on historical data, without the ability to dynamically adapt to real-time information. They are slow to process new data inputs, often requiring months or even years of adjustment before accurately reflecting reality. Moreover, these models struggle with complex data sets where multiple variables interact in unexpected ways. In a world where macroeconomic trends can be influenced by factors as disparate as climate change, geopolitical tensions, and technological innovations, static econometric frameworks are increasingly inadequate.

This is where AI steps in as a game changer. Unlike traditional models, AI-based forecasting systems can learn from vast, multifaceted data sets, identify non-obvious patterns, and dynamically update predictions based on new information. With AI, economic forecasting transforms from a reactive science to a proactive, predictive art, marked by unprecedented precision and speed.

How AI Is Transforming Economic Forecasting

The essence of AI's transformative power lies in its ability to handle and make sense of big data. Global economies generate staggering volumes of data every second, from financial markets and consumer behavior to international trade flows and social media activity. Traditional economists would be overwhelmed by the sheer quantity and variety of this data. AI, however, thrives in complexity. Through advanced machine learning algorithms, AI can analyze enormous data sets, recognizing subtle correlations and patterns that human analysts might overlook.

Take, for example, the use of AI in predicting consumer spending behavior. Machine learning models can process data from credit card transactions, online search trends, social media discussions, and real-time economic indicators to forecast retail sales more accurately than traditional regression models. By incorporating non-traditional data sources – such as sentiment analysis from social media – AI provides a richer, more nuanced view of consumer confidence, capturing the subtleties of economic behavior that traditional metrics often miss.

AI-driven models excel in scenario analysis and stress testing. These methods simulate the potential impact of extreme or unlikely events on economies, helping businesses and policymakers plan for a range of outcomes. For instance, an AI system might analyze how a geopolitical event, like a sudden oil price shock, could ripple through global markets. This capability allows decision-makers to develop more robust strategies and mitigate potential risks.

The implications for central banks are equally profound. Monetary authorities have traditionally relied on models with lagging indicators to set interest rates and guide fiscal policy. AI, however, introduces a forward-looking perspective. Central banks can use machine learning to anticipate inflation trends or employment shifts with greater accuracy, thus responding faster to economic changes. The Federal Reserve and the European Central Bank have already begun experimenting with AI-based approaches to refine their economic forecasting processes, highlighting AI's increasing role in shaping global monetary policy.

Case Study: AI in Action – Predicting Economic Shifts

One of the most compelling examples of AI's power in economic forecasting comes from the investment industry. Hedge funds and asset managers have embraced AI to gain an edge in predicting financial market movements. Take Bridgewater Associates, one of the world's largest hedge funds, which employs AI algorithms to process a plethora of economic data and generate actionable investment strategies. These algorithms analyze everything from labor market data and international trade balances to Twitter sentiment and satellite imagery of global shipping lanes.

Imagine the complexity of forecasting oil prices. Traditional models might consider supply and demand fundamentals, along with OPEC's production targets. An AI-based model, however, takes a vastly more comprehensive approach. It can analyze geopolitical news feeds, predict potential disruptions in supply routes, assess weather patterns affecting oil fields, and monitor global inventory levels using satellite images. The result? Faster and more accurate oil price forecasts, empowering traders and energy companies to make informed decisions in real time.

Another groundbreaking application of AI is in currency exchange forecasting. In the world of forex trading, where market dynamics can shift within seconds, speed and precision are vital. AI models analyze cross-border trade data, interest rate differentials, central bank policies, and even social media sentiment to predict currency movements. They can execute trades in milliseconds, outperforming human traders and traditional algorithms that are slow to adapt to new data. For multinational corporations, these AI insights help optimize hedging strategies and reduce exposure to currency risk.

Beyond Predictive Accuracy – The Strategic Advantage of AI

The strategic advantages of AI in economic forecasting extend beyond predictive accuracy. For businesses and investors, speed is a critical differentiator. In a hyper-competitive environment, being able to anticipate economic shifts faster than competitors can translate into significant financial gains. AI-driven models provide that edge, delivering forecasts in real time and empowering decision-makers to act swiftly.

Consider the strategic benefits for supply chain management. AI models can predict disruptions caused by geopolitical events or natural disasters, allowing companies to adjust sourcing strategies or inventory levels preemptively. During the pandemic, companies that used AI to forecast supply chain bottlenecks were able to adapt more efficiently, mitigating losses and ensuring product availability. This level of agility is invaluable, especially in a world where supply chain vulnerabilities are increasingly visible and costly.

AI's speed and precision are revolutionizing risk management in the financial sector. Banks use AI to monitor credit risk and predict loan defaults with extraordinary accuracy. By analyzing not only borrowers' financial histories but also real-time economic conditions, AI models offer early warnings of potential risks, helping institutions mitigate losses. This is particularly crucial for developing economies, where traditional credit assessment methods often fail to account for informal labor markets and other complexities. AI provides a more inclusive and accurate approach to assessing economic risk in diverse environments.

Policymakers also stand to benefit enormously from AI-enhanced forecasting. Economic policy decisions often rely on forecasts that are months old, a delay that can have severe repercussions. With AI, policymakers can receive real-time updates on economic conditions, enabling more proactive and effective interventions. For instance, AI could help anticipate the economic impact of climate change, guiding investments in infrastructure and green technologies. As governments around the world grapple with increasingly complex economic challenges, the ability to forecast accurately and act swiftly will become ever more critical.

Challenges and Ethical Considerations

Despite the immense promise of AI in economic forecasting, it is not without challenges. One of the primary concerns is the "black box" problem – the lack of transparency in how AI algorithms make decisions. This opacity can be problematic, especially when economic forecasts influence major policy decisions or investment strategies. If AI makes a prediction that turns out to be incorrect, understanding why the model failed is crucial. Economists and data scientists are working to develop more interpretable AI models, but striking the balance between complexity and transparency remains a formidable challenge.

Data quality is another significant issue. AI models are only as good as the data they are trained on. Inconsistent or biased data can lead to skewed forecasts, with potentially disastrous consequences. For example, if an AI system relies heavily on data from developed economies, it may not accurately predict trends in emerging markets. Ensuring that AI models are trained on diverse and high-quality data is vital for their success.

Ethical considerations around data privacy and algorithmic bias cannot be ignored. The use of personal data in AI-driven forecasting raises questions about surveillance and individual privacy. Policymakers must establish clear guidelines to protect citizens' rights while allowing for technological innovation. Additionally, there is a risk that AI models could exacerbate existing inequalities. For instance, if AI-driven economic policies disproportionately benefit wealthy nations or corporations, it could deepen global economic disparities.

Embracing AI's Potential While Navigating Its Challenges

AI is not a panacea for all the complexities of economic forecasting, but it is undoubtedly a powerful tool that offers unparalleled precision and speed. By embracing AI, economists, businesses, and policymakers can move from reactive to proactive decision-making, unlocking new possibilities in the management of economic risk and opportunity. However, as we harness AI's potential, we must also address the ethical and practical challenges it presents. Transparency, data quality, and equitable access to AI technology will be crucial factors in ensuring that this revolution benefits society as a whole.

As we move forward into an era defined by data and complexity, the future of economic forecasting lies in our ability to integrate human ingenuity with the computational power of AI. The synergy between traditional economic expertise and cutting-edge technology will shape a world where forecasts are not just more accurate but also more impactful, empowering us to navigate an unpredictable global economy with greater confidence and resilience.

Challenges in AI-Driven Economic Forecasting

Despite its revolutionary potential, the integration of AI into economic forecasting is not without significant hurdles. As AI algorithms become more embedded in predictive models, a trio of prominent issues has surfaced: the opacity of AI models, data quality concerns, and ethical dilemmas surrounding bias and fairness. Understanding these challenges is crucial for a balanced assessment of AI's role in transforming economic forecasting.

1. The Opacity and "Black Box" Problem

One of the most prominent challenges associated with AI in economic forecasting is the opacity, or "black box," nature of many machine learning models. Deep learning algorithms, for example, are often so complex that even their creators struggle to explain how they arrive at specific conclusions. This lack of transparency raises critical questions when it comes to interpreting AI-driven economic forecasts. For policymakers, businesses, and investors who rely on these forecasts to make high-stakes decisions, not understanding the reasoning behind a prediction can be problematic.

Consider, for instance, a scenario where an AI model predicts a significant economic downturn within the next quarter. If the forecast prompts a government to implement emergency economic measures, but the AI model's prediction turns out to be erroneous, the costs could be catastrophic. A case in point is the AI-driven predictions used by hedge funds: while these algorithms often outperform traditional analysis, they are not infallible. During the 2020 market crash triggered by the COVID-19 pandemic, some AI models failed to predict the extent of the economic shock, and their rapid, unexplained decisions exacerbated market volatility.

Research by PwC estimates that AI could contribute up to $15.7 trillion to the global economy by 2030, but it also warns that explainability remains one of the critical barriers to widespread AI adoption in sectors like finance . In economic policy, where trust and transparency are paramount, the "black box" problem is a major obstacle. The inability to provide clear justifications for AI-driven forecasts undermines the credibility of these systems and complicates their integration into mainstream economic analysis.

2. Data Quality and Availability

AI models thrive on data, but the quality and availability of such data often present a formidable challenge. Economic forecasting requires vast amounts of information from diverse sources, including labor statistics, trade data, consumer behavior metrics, and financial transactions. If this data is inconsistent, incomplete, or outdated, the AI models built on it can generate misleading or inaccurate predictions. Moreover, data silos and proprietary ownership restrict access to comprehensive data sets, limiting the effectiveness of AI-driven forecasting.

For example, in developing economies, where reliable economic data is often sparse or unavailable, AI models may produce forecasts that are heavily skewed or unreliable. This issue is not hypothetical. A study conducted by the Brookings Institution found that AI models predicting agricultural productivity in Africa performed poorly compared to models used in Europe and North America, primarily due to a lack of quality data from the region . Such disparities highlight the urgent need to invest in better data infrastructure and make economic data more universally accessible.

Furthermore, data quality issues are compounded by the challenge of integrating non-traditional data sources, such as social media sentiment or satellite imagery. While these sources provide valuable insights, they often contain noise and inconsistencies that AI algorithms must learn to filter. Even sophisticated AI models can struggle with this, making the process of data curation and cleaning as critical as the algorithms themselves. Inaccurate data inputs lead to flawed outputs, underscoring the age-old adage in data science: "garbage in, garbage out."

3. Ethical and Fairness Concerns

The third major problem associated with AI-driven economic forecasting is the issue of fairness and ethics. AI models are susceptible to biases, which can emerge from the data they are trained on or from the way algorithms are designed. When it comes to economic forecasting, biased predictions can have far-reaching implications, disproportionately affecting vulnerable populations or reinforcing existing inequalities. This challenge raises questions about the fairness and ethical use of AI in economic contexts.

For instance, consider an AI model used to forecast unemployment rates. If the training data reflects historical labor market discrimination, the AI may inadvertently reinforce these patterns, predicting higher unemployment rates for marginalized groups. Such biased forecasts could influence government policies, potentially perpetuating social and economic disparities. The problem becomes even more pronounced when AI models are used to assess credit risk in banking. According to a 2021 report by the Center for Data Innovation, AI-driven credit scoring models have occasionally demonstrated racial biases, leading to unfair lending practices .

These ethical dilemmas have sparked global debates about how to ensure fairness and accountability in AI systems. Governments and regulatory bodies are now grappling with the question of how to create guidelines that balance innovation with social responsibility. For economic forecasting, this means that models must be not only accurate but also equitable, providing predictions that consider diverse economic realities without exacerbating inequalities.

Opportunities in AI-Driven Economic Forecasting

Despite these challenges, AI's potential to revolutionize economic forecasting presents a wealth of opportunities. If implemented thoughtfully, AI can significantly enhance the accuracy, efficiency, and inclusiveness of economic predictions. Here, we explore three transformative opportunities: enhanced precision and adaptability, proactive economic interventions, and democratized access to economic insights.

1. Enhanced Precision and Adaptability

One of the most compelling opportunities presented by AI is the potential for enhanced precision and adaptability in economic forecasting. Traditional econometric models often struggle to adjust to real-time changes, but AI systems can continually learn and adapt. By processing new data in real-time and recognizing patterns that evolve over time, AI can provide forecasts that are not only more accurate but also more responsive to sudden shifts.

For example, in the retail sector, companies like Walmart and Amazon have leveraged AI to optimize inventory management based on economic forecasts. During the holiday season, these AI models analyze consumer spending patterns, supply chain data, and economic indicators to predict demand spikes with remarkable accuracy. A 2023 report from McKinsey highlighted that retailers using AI-based forecasting saw inventory-related costs decrease by 20% while improving stock availability by up to 30% . This kind of precision is transforming supply chain management and helping businesses mitigate economic risks.

Beyond retail, central banks are beginning to experiment with AI models to predict inflation and GDP growth. The Bank of England, for instance, has developed machine learning tools that analyze real-time data from various sectors to forecast economic trends more dynamically. These advancements allow monetary policymakers to respond more quickly to economic shifts, enhancing the overall stability of the financial system. AI's adaptability is a key advantage, providing economic forecasts that can adjust to a rapidly changing global landscape.

2. Proactive Economic Interventions

AI-driven economic forecasting also enables more proactive economic interventions. Traditional forecasting methods often lead to reactive policies, where governments and businesses address economic issues only after they have manifested. AI, however, provides the foresight needed to implement preventive measures, mitigating economic shocks before they become crises. This proactive approach can have profound effects on economic stability and growth.

Consider the agricultural sector, where climate-related risks pose a significant threat. AI models can predict droughts or floods months in advance by analyzing weather patterns, soil data, and historical climate trends. This information allows governments and farmers to take preventive measures, such as adjusting irrigation strategies or diversifying crops. The World Bank has invested in AI projects that help farmers in Africa and Asia forecast climate-related risks, with early results showing a 15-20% increase in agricultural productivity due to better planning and risk mitigation.

In the financial sector, AI's predictive capabilities can also help regulators identify systemic risks before they become widespread crises. By analyzing vast amounts of financial data, AI can detect emerging vulnerabilities in banking systems, such as overleveraged institutions or signs of market bubbles. This foresight enables regulators to act early, implementing measures to prevent economic meltdowns. The 2008 financial crisis demonstrated the need for such proactive oversight, and AI offers the tools to make this vision a reality.

3. Democratized Access to Economic Insights

The third significant opportunity lies in democratizing access to economic insights. In the past, high-quality economic forecasts were often reserved for large financial institutions and governments with the resources to invest in advanced econometric models. AI has the potential to change this by making economic forecasting tools more accessible and affordable for a wider range of users, including small businesses, startups, and even individual entrepreneurs.

Startups like Quandl and DataRobot are already offering AI-driven economic forecasting platforms that small businesses can use to make informed decisions. For instance, a small e-commerce company can use AI tools to predict consumer spending trends, enabling more strategic marketing and inventory planning. This democratization of economic insights levels the playing field, allowing smaller players to compete with larger corporations. A 2022 report from Gartner found that companies using democratized AI forecasting solutions experienced a 15% increase in revenue growth compared to those relying on traditional methods.

AI-driven platforms can provide localized economic forecasts, empowering communities and small municipalities to make data-driven decisions. For instance, a city government could use AI to predict the economic impact of infrastructure projects or demographic shifts, optimizing resource allocation for maximum benefit. This increased accessibility to economic forecasting not only fosters innovation but also ensures that a broader segment of society can harness the power of predictive analytics.

Balancing Challenges with Opportunities

The integration of AI into economic forecasting is a double-edged sword, presenting both formidable challenges and groundbreaking opportunities. The "black box" nature of AI models, data quality concerns, and ethical issues around bias are serious obstacles that must be addressed. However, the benefits – including enhanced precision, proactive economic planning, and democratized access to economic insights – offer a promising vision for the future.

Navigating this landscape will require a concerted effort from policymakers, businesses, and the tech community. Investing in transparent and interpretable AI systems, improving data infrastructure, and establishing ethical guidelines will be crucial steps in ensuring that AI serves as a force for good in economic forecasting. As we embrace these technologies, the ultimate goal should be to create a more resilient, equitable, and informed global economy.

CHAPTER 3: STRATEGIC BUSINESS MANAGEMENT – LEVERAGING AI FOR COMPETITIVE EDGE

Key Questions for the Reader:

1. How can artificial intelligence transform strategic business management to achieve unparalleled competitive advantage?

2. What are the most innovative ways AI is being utilized to optimize decision-making in business?

3. How can your organization adapt and implement AI strategies effectively to remain competitive in a fast-evolving market?

The business landscape today is defined by rapid technological advancements and fierce competition. In this environment, traditional business management practices are increasingly insufficient to maintain growth and competitive advantage. Enter artificial intelligence (AI) — a technology not only revolutionizing the way organizations operate but redefining strategic business management altogether. From predictive analytics and automation to personalized customer experiences, AI's integration into strategic frameworks offers transformative potential for businesses aiming to stand out in a saturated market.

1. The Evolution of Strategic Business Management in the AI Era

Strategic business management has traditionally focused on long-term goals, resource allocation, and competitive positioning. However, with the rise of AI, this discipline has undergone a metamorphosis. No longer is it solely about forecasting based on historical data or following rigid five-year plans. Today, AI-infused strategies emphasize agility, real-time insights, and proactive decision-making.

AI enables leaders to not just respond to industry trends but to anticipate them. By processing vast amounts of data with machine learning (ML) algorithms, organizations can identify patterns and trends that would be imperceptible through human analysis alone. For instance, AI-powered tools like IBM Watson or Salesforce Einstein assist executives in strategic planning by offering actionable intelligence derived from big data.

2. Enhancing Decision-Making with AI: The Cognitive Boost

Strategic decision-making is the backbone of successful management. AI enhances this by providing cognitive support through advanced analytics and predictive models. These capabilities empower business leaders to make data-driven decisions that are not only informed but also more precise.

For example, AI-driven analytics platforms like Tableau and Power BI have integrated machine learning features that enable managers to forecast future market conditions, simulate scenarios, and optimize operations. This aids in minimizing risk and maximizing opportunities. Moreover, natural language processing (NLP) tools enable the extraction of valuable insights from unstructured data such as customer reviews, social media discussions, and industry reports, ensuring that decision-making is comprehensive and reflective of current market sentiments.

3. Automation and Efficiency: Transforming Operational Strategies

Automation, a subset of AI, is revolutionizing operational management by performing repetitive tasks more efficiently than humans. Robotic Process Automation (RPA) tools such as UiPath and Blue Prism can handle tasks ranging from data entry to customer support, freeing up human resources for higher-value work. This not only reduces errors but enhances productivity and job satisfaction by allowing employees to focus on more strategic and creative tasks.

Take, for example, the financial sector where AI-driven bots process transactions, detect fraudulent activity, and ensure compliance with regulations. These advancements reduce operational costs and help maintain an agile and resilient business model. For any company seeking to scale its operations without exponentially increasing overheads, strategic implementation of AI in process automation is a key differentiator.

4. AI-Driven Personalization: Revolutionizing Customer Engagement

The future of competitive advantage lies in how well a business understands and engages its customers. AI enables hyper-personalization — tailoring products, services, and marketing to individual preferences on a scale previously unimaginable. Algorithms analyze user behavior and feedback in real-time to create bespoke experiences. For instance, AI platforms like Adobe Sensei help businesses craft personalized content that resonates with specific audiences, enhancing customer loyalty and conversion rates.

Retail giants like Amazon and Netflix have set the standard by harnessing AI for recommendation systems that significantly increase user engagement and sales. These tailored experiences are not exclusive to tech behemoths; small and medium enterprises (SMEs) can also leverage AI tools for personalized email campaigns, dynamic website experiences, and adaptive customer service solutions.

5. Competitive Analysis and Market Intelligence

One of AI's most compelling contributions to strategic management is its ability to automate and deepen market research. Machine learning algorithms can process data from competitors, industry reports, and financial records to identify competitive advantages and gaps in the market. Tools like Crayon and Klue provide competitive intelligence by tracking competitors' activities, including product launches, marketing strategies, and pricing changes.

This form of augmented intelligence allows businesses to react swiftly to competitive moves and adjust their strategies in real-time. Companies no longer have to rely solely on annual or quarterly analysis; they can leverage AI to continuously monitor and adapt their strategic positioning.

6. Building an AI-Ready Culture and Workforce

Implementing AI in strategic business management goes beyond technology; it requires a cultural shift. An AI-ready organization is one that not only integrates advanced tools but also promotes a culture of innovation, continuous learning, and agility. Business leaders must prioritize training and upskilling employees to work alongside AI, turning them into strategic partners of technology rather than just users.

Programs that focus on developing data literacy, ethical considerations in AI usage, and collaborative problem-solving skills are essential. For instance, Google's AI workshops and MIT's AI courses for business leaders help cultivate an understanding of how AI tools function and how they can be applied effectively in decision-making.

7. Ethical and Regulatory Considerations in AI Strategy

As AI adoption grows, so does the scrutiny around its ethical use and regulatory compliance. Strategic business management must consider the impact of AI on privacy, job displacement, and bias in algorithms. Ensuring that AI applications are aligned with ethical principles not only safeguards a company's reputation but also minimizes the risk of regulatory fines and public backlash.

Developing AI with transparency and fairness involves practices such as explainable AI (XAI), which makes the decision-making processes of algorithms understandable to humans. Furthermore, adhering to regulations like the European Union's GDPR (General Data Protection Regulation) or the emerging AI-specific guidelines ensures that a business remains compliant while utilizing AI to its fullest potential.

8. Implementing AI Strategies: Best Practices and Roadmap

Integrating AI into strategic business management requires careful planning and execution. The following roadmap outlines best practices for successful AI implementation:

- Assessment and Goal Setting: Identify areas within the business where AI can have the most significant impact. Establish clear objectives for AI use, whether it's enhancing customer experience, optimizing operations, or developing new products.

- Data Strategy: Ensure that the organization has a robust data infrastructure capable of supporting AI. This includes not only gathering high-quality data but also maintaining its security and privacy.

- Pilot Programs: Start small with pilot projects to test AI solutions in a controlled environment. This allows businesses to learn, adapt, and scale successful initiatives.

- Collaboration with AI Experts: Engage with AI specialists and data scientists to build or customize AI models that fit the company's unique needs.

- Continuous Monitoring and Adjustment: AI applications should be continuously monitored for performance and improved based on feedback and changing business requirements.

9. Case Studies: Real-World Applications of AI in Strategic Business Management

A look at how leading companies have harnessed AI for competitive advantage highlights its power:

- Spotify: The music streaming giant uses AI not just to recommend songs but to develop strategic partnerships and market its services more effectively. By analyzing listening data, the company makes data-driven decisions on expanding its playlist curation and collaborations with artists.

- BMW: In the automotive industry, BMW leverages AI to streamline production processes, improve quality control, and deliver a personalized customer experience. AI in their manufacturing helps predict maintenance needs, reducing downtime and enhancing efficiency.

- Healthcare Startups: Companies like Tempus and Zebra Medical Vision utilize AI for predictive analytics and diagnostics. By processing large volumes of medical data, these startups provide insights that shape healthcare strategies, optimize treatment plans, and drive competitive advantage.

The competitive edge that AI provides is more than just a temporary advantage; it is a shift in how strategic business management is approached. Organizations that embrace AI not just as a tool, but as a strategic partner, will navigate market complexities with a sharper, more informed perspective. The real winners in the coming decade will be those who leverage AI not just to keep pace but to set the pace in their respective industries.

AI's role in business management is still evolving, but its current applications already show tremendous potential. The time is now for businesses to evaluate their strategies, invest in AI capabilities, and build a resilient future prepared for technological advancements. Embracing AI means more than integrating technology; it's about reimagining the core of business strategy itself.

The Chronology and Key Milestones of AI in Strategic Business Management – Past, Present, and Future

The journey of artificial intelligence (AI) in strategic business management is a testament to the evolution of technology, marked by significant milestones that have reshaped industries. From rudimentary automation to sophisticated AI-driven analytics, the story of AI has been one of exponential growth and adaptation. This chapter explores the chronological development of AI, highlights key achievements, and forecasts its future potential. Additionally, we will delve into how two leading companies have excelled in strategically integrating AI into their business models, providing concrete examples and figures.

1. The Origins of AI in Business: Setting the Stage

The roots of AI can be traced back to the mid-20th century, when computer scientists like Alan Turing and John McCarthy laid the groundwork for artificial intelligence as a concept. However, the initial application of AI in business was limited by the technological capabilities of the era.

1950s–1970s: The Dawn of AI

In the early years, AI research was largely academic and focused on developing algorithms that could mimic human problem-solving. The introduction of simple computer programs that could play chess or solve mathematical puzzles represented the first use cases of AI, but their application in business was minimal. Companies began to experiment with data processing systems that could automate basic tasks, but these systems lacked the sophistication required for strategic decision-making.

1980s–1990s: The Era of Expert Systems

The 1980s marked a significant milestone with the rise of expert systems, designed to simulate human decision-making within specific domains. These systems allowed businesses to automate some aspects of operations and decision-making processes. For example, early adopters in the finance sector began using rule-based systems to support decision-making in credit scoring and fraud detection.

A notable example from this era is the use of AI in logistics. Companies like DHL began using computerized systems to optimize routes and manage inventory, setting the stage for more complex applications in the future. However, these systems were limited by their reliance on pre-defined rules and lacked the ability to adapt or learn from new data.

2000s: The Advent of Machine Learning

The 2000s ushered in the age of machine learning (ML), a paradigm shift that allowed AI to learn from data and improve its performance over time. This change was driven by the exponential growth of data and advances in computing power. Machine learning models could now process and analyze vast amounts of information, providing businesses with predictive insights that informed strategic management.

One of the most impactful milestones during this period was the emergence of AI-powered analytics tools. For instance, Amazon pioneered the use of AI in its recommendation system, which significantly boosted sales and set a new standard for customer personalization. By analyzing user behavior, preferences, and purchase history, Amazon's algorithms could suggest products that matched customer interests, contributing to an increase in sales by 29% in just a few years.

2. The Present: AI as a Core Business Strategy

Today, AI has become a central pillar in strategic business management, transforming industries through its ability to analyze data, automate processes, and personalize experiences. This era is characterized by real-time data processing, the use of advanced algorithms, and the integration of AI in all facets of business operations.

AI in Financial Services

In the financial sector, AI-driven tools like JPMorgan Chase's COiN (Contract Intelligence) platform can process 12,000 commercial credit agreements in seconds, a task that previously required 360,000 hours of manual labor. This not only saves significant time and cost but also reduces the risk of human error.

AI in Supply Chain Management

Companies are also leveraging AI to optimize supply chain strategies. Siemens, for example, has integrated AI to predict equipment failures before they happen. Their predictive maintenance strategies have reduced downtime by up to 50%, ensuring smoother operations and significant cost savings.

Case Study 1: Tesla – Redefining the Automotive Industry

Tesla is a prime example of a company using AI not just as a tool but as a fundamental aspect of its business strategy. Tesla's autopilot system, powered by neural networks, represents one of the most advanced uses of AI in real-world applications. It processes data from millions of vehicles to improve its self-driving capabilities. In 2023, Tesla reported that their AI systems contributed to a 20% reduction in production costs through more efficient automation and predictive maintenance.

Additionally, Tesla's Dojo supercomputer is designed to train its autonomous systems at scale, allowing the company to iterate on AI models faster than its competitors. The integration of AI into its strategy has positioned Tesla not just as an automaker but as a tech innovator, drawing significant market interest and investor confidence. In 2022, Tesla's market capitalization soared past $1 trillion, a testament to its strategic embrace of AI.

Case Study 2: Microsoft – Driving Business Solutions with AI

Microsoft has emerged as a leader in the strategic implementation of AI through its cloud-based AI services and platforms like Azure AI. By integrating AI into Microsoft 365, the company has enhanced productivity tools such as Word and Excel with features like automated data analysis, predictive text, and intelligent task prioritization. According to a 2022 report, these enhancements boosted productivity by an average of 15% for enterprise users.

Moreover, Microsoft's acquisition of OpenAI's technology has enabled the development of Copilot—a tool integrated within its products that leverages generative AI to assist users in drafting documents, coding, and data visualization. This seamless integration of AI has reinforced Microsoft's position as a leader in the enterprise software market, which contributed to a 20% increase in their annual cloud revenue, surpassing $90 billion in 2023.

3. The Future: AI as the Strategic Navigator

The future of AI in strategic business management holds promise as new innovations push the boundaries of what AI can achieve. Key trends shaping the future include increased personalization, deeper human-AI collaboration, and enhanced ethical considerations.

Hyper-Personalization and Predictive Insights

The next decade will see an even more refined approach to personalization. AI algorithms will evolve to understand not just user preferences but context and intent at a granular level. This will allow businesses to anticipate customer needs before they are expressed, leading to higher customer retention and brand loyalty. Companies that harness this will find themselves steps ahead in competitive markets.

Human-AI Symbiosis in the Workforce

The future of strategic business management will involve closer integration between human expertise and AI. Augmented decision-making tools will help executives simulate scenarios with even greater precision, accounting for variables like global supply chain disruptions or economic shifts. This collaboration is expected to improve decision-making efficiency by 30% over the next five years.

Ethics and Regulatory Challenges

As AI becomes more central to business strategies, ethical and regulatory considerations will grow in importance. Companies must balance innovation with ethical AI use to ensure fairness, transparency, and accountability. Regulatory bodies around the world are already crafting AI-specific legislation aimed at preventing bias and protecting consumer privacy.

Projected Growth and Economic Impact

According to a PwC study, AI could contribute up to $15.7 trillion to the global economy by 2030, driven by productivity gains and increased consumer demand. Businesses that proactively adopt AI strategies are expected to see revenue growth at nearly double the rate of non-adopters.

4. Strategic Excellence: Two Companies Leading the Charge

Among the global leaders, Tesla and Microsoft stand out for their exemplary management and integration of AI.

Tesla's Strategic Mastery

Tesla's approach goes beyond automotive innovation. The company's AI capabilities extend to energy solutions and AI-driven manufacturing. By integrating machine learning models into its Gigafactories, Tesla optimizes production processes, enabling the rapid scaling of output to meet global demand. The result has been a consistent 50% year-over-year production growth.

Microsoft's AI-Driven Ecosystem

Microsoft's holistic strategy of embedding AI into its ecosystem—from enterprise solutions to consumer products—illustrates how businesses can transform operations and achieve substantial growth. The company's collaboration with OpenAI has bolstered its competitive edge, positioning it at the forefront of generative AI technologies. Their strategic approach, which includes the democratization of AI through accessible platforms, has cemented their leadership in the market.

The journey of AI in strategic business management—from basic algorithms to complex, learning-based systems—illustrates the incredible potential of this technology. Companies that have effectively integrated AI into their business strategies have not only enhanced efficiency and profitability but also set new standards for industry practices. As AI continues to evolve, organizations must remain vigilant, agile, and committed to ethical standards to harness its full potential. The future holds vast opportunities for those willing to invest in AI not just as a tool but as an essential strategic partner.

Period	Milestone/Development	Example Company	Impact/Key Figures
1950s–1970s	Initial AI concepts and algorithms	N/A	Academic applications; early basic automations.
1980s–1990s	Expert systems in business	DHL	Route and inventory optimization; early AI applications in logistics.
2000s	Emergence of machine learning	Amazon	Implementation of recommendation systems; sales increased by 29%.
2010s	Advanced integration of AI and Big Data	JPMorgan Chase	COiN platform reduced 360,000 hours of manual work to seconds.
2020s	Expansion of AI in personalization and productivity	Microsoft	Microsoft 365 with AI boosted productivity by 15%; Azure AI contributed to $90 billion in revenue by 2023.
2023	Advanced AI application in production	Tesla	20% reduction in production costs; 50% annual production growth.
Future (2030)	Predictions and new applications	Various (predictions)	AI could contribute up to $15.7 trillion to the global economy; business productivity expected to increase by 30%.

CHAPTER 4: NAVIGATING ETHICAL AI – RESPONSIBLE IMPLEMENTATION IN GLOBAL BUSINESS

In today's dynamic global economy, Artificial Intelligence (AI) has emerged as a powerful catalyst for innovation and efficiency, fundamentally reshaping financial markets, economic policies, and business strategies. However, as AI's influence expands, so too does the imperative for ethical oversight. Ethical AI is not just a compliance requirement but a strategic necessity for sustainable and responsible global business practices. This chapter explores how companies can successfully navigate the complex ethical landscape of AI, ensuring responsible implementation that not only maximizes value but also builds trust among stakeholders.

4.1 Understanding the Ethical Imperatives of AI

The deployment of AI technology in business and finance must be informed by a nuanced understanding of ethical principles. These principles ensure that AI contributes positively to society, avoids exacerbating inequalities, and respects fundamental human rights. At the core of ethical AI are several key considerations: fairness, transparency, accountability, and the minimization of bias.

1. Fairness and Non-Discrimination

AI systems often reflect the biases of the data they are trained on. When companies implement AI models for credit scoring, hiring processes, or risk assessment, these models may inadvertently perpetuate societal inequities if they rely on biased data. For example, a predictive algorithm that has been trained on historical data might unfairly penalize minority communities if historical inequities are not corrected. Responsible AI implementation, therefore, requires constant auditing and refinement of algorithms to ensure they treat all demographics equitably.

2. Transparency and Explainability

The "black box" nature of many AI models poses a significant challenge. Businesses and regulators need to understand how AI-driven decisions are made, especially in high-stakes domains like finance or healthcare. Explainability ensures that AI systems operate transparently, and it allows stakeholders to comprehend the rationale behind automated decisions. Moreover, in cases where AI impacts consumers directly, such as loan approvals or personalized pricing, explainability is key to fostering trust and mitigating backlash.

3. Accountability and Governance

Ethical AI also demands clear accountability structures. Who is responsible when an AI-driven system makes a faulty or harmful decision? Businesses must develop governance frameworks that clearly delineate accountability, ensuring that human oversight remains integral to AI deployment. This might include establishing ethical review boards, appointing AI ethics officers, or implementing regular audits to monitor AI system performance.

4.2 The Global Business Case for Ethical AI

Implementing ethical AI is not just a matter of social responsibility; it is a strategic business imperative. As AI technology becomes more pervasive, public scrutiny and regulatory pressures are increasing. Companies that prioritize ethical AI are better positioned to mitigate risks and capitalize on the opportunities AI presents.

1. Regulatory Compliance and Anticipating Legislation

Regulatory frameworks for AI are rapidly evolving. The European Union's AI Act, for instance, aims to establish rules for AI that prioritize human rights and consumer safety. Companies that proactively align with these regulations can avoid costly fines and legal challenges. By adopting best practices early, businesses can also influence regulatory standards and position themselves as leaders in the ethical AI movement.

2. Reputation Management and Brand Value

Trust is a crucial currency in the modern business landscape. Companies that are perceived as ethical and responsible in their AI practices can strengthen their brand reputation. This, in turn, can lead to increased consumer loyalty and a competitive edge in the market. On the flip side, ethical lapses—such as discriminatory AI models or data privacy breaches—can lead to reputational damage and loss of consumer confidence.

3. Driving Long-Term Value Creation

Ethical AI implementation fosters innovation and resilience. By integrating ethics into AI strategies, companies can identify new opportunities to create value while mitigating risks. For example, AI-driven supply chain models that consider ethical sourcing and labor standards can attract socially conscious investors and customers. Furthermore, responsible

AI practices can help businesses anticipate societal trends and align their operations with evolving consumer expectations.

4.3 Practical Frameworks for Ethical AI Implementation

To navigate the ethical complexities of AI, businesses need robust frameworks that guide responsible implementation. This involves adopting a multidisciplinary approach that brings together expertise from data science, ethics, law, and business strategy.

1. AI Ethics Guidelines and Policies

A foundational step is to establish comprehensive AI ethics guidelines. These guidelines should articulate the company's commitment to ethical AI and outline principles for AI development and deployment. Effective guidelines are not static; they evolve as new challenges and insights emerge. Companies like Google and Microsoft have set precedents by publishing their AI ethics principles, which emphasize fairness, transparency, and respect for user privacy.

2. Bias Auditing and Mitigation

To combat algorithmic bias, businesses must invest in rigorous auditing mechanisms. This includes testing AI models across diverse demographic groups to identify potential disparities. Techniques such as re-sampling training data, incorporating fairness constraints into model design, and conducting third-party reviews can help mitigate bias. Additionally, businesses should foster diversity in their AI development teams to bring varied perspectives that reduce the risk of blind spots.

3. Transparency and Communication

Businesses should strive to make AI systems as interpretable as possible. This can involve using simpler models where feasible, providing detailed documentation, or developing user-friendly interfaces that explain AI decisions in layman's terms. Effective communication is especially important in industries like healthcare and finance, where the stakes of AI decisions are high. Additionally, engaging with stakeholders—ranging from customers to regulatory bodies—can ensure that AI practices are aligned with societal expectations.

4.4 Ethical AI in Practice: Case Studies and Lessons Learned

Several companies and organizations have successfully integrated ethical AI practices, providing valuable insights into what works and what doesn't.

1. Financial Services: Bias and Fair Lending

In the financial sector, AI is transforming risk assessment, fraud detection, and customer service. However, ethical challenges abound, especially regarding lending decisions. A leading example is the case of a major bank that deployed an AI-driven credit scoring system. Initial models were found to disadvantage certain racial and socioeconomic groups, prompting the bank to overhaul its approach. By working with AI ethicists and conducting ongoing audits, the bank developed a fairer, more transparent model that met regulatory standards and improved customer satisfaction.

2. Healthcare: Balancing Innovation and Patient Safety

In healthcare, AI systems are used for diagnostics, treatment recommendations, and operational efficiency. One prominent case involved an AI system designed to predict patient outcomes. The algorithm showed promising results but was later criticized for prioritizing efficiency over patient safety. The healthcare provider responded by forming an AI ethics board and ensuring that clinicians had the final say in patient care decisions. This experience highlighted the importance of human oversight and the need for ethical guardrails in high-stakes environments.

3. Consumer Technology: Privacy and User Consent

Consumer technology companies often face challenges related to data privacy and user consent. A well-known tech company faced backlash after users discovered their personal data was being used without clear consent. In response, the company implemented stricter data governance practices, anonymized user data, and developed a more transparent user consent process. This case underscores the significance of respecting user privacy and being transparent about data usage.

4.5 Future Outlook: The Road to Ethical AI Excellence

The journey toward ethical AI is ongoing and requires continuous adaptation. As AI technology evolves, so will the ethical challenges. Businesses must remain agile, proactive, and committed to ethical principles. Emerging trends, such as the rise of AI ethics certifications, the integration of AI ethics in university curricula, and the development of AI ethics-as-a-service platforms, indicate a promising future for ethical AI.

To stay ahead, businesses should foster a culture of ethical awareness, invest in AI literacy programs, and engage in collaborative initiatives that drive industry-wide progress. Ultimately, ethical AI is about balancing innovation with responsibility, ensuring that AI technology serves humanity's best interests while driving economic and strategic success.

Navigating ethical AI is a strategic journey that requires robust frameworks, interdisciplinary collaboration, and a genuine commitment to doing what is right. By prioritizing ethics in AI implementation, global businesses can unlock the transformative potential of AI in a manner that is sustainable, equitable, and beneficial to all stakeholders.

AI-Driven Financial Forecasting Models – Three Innovative Approaches for Ethical and Responsible Financial Control

In the fast-evolving global business landscape, Artificial Intelligence (AI) is revolutionizing financial forecasting and control. Accurate financial projections are vital for strategic decision-making, risk management, and efficient capital allocation. However, the introduction of AI-based forecasting models introduces new ethical considerations that must be managed thoughtfully. This chapter delves into three AI-driven forecasting models designed to optimize financial outcomes while adhering to responsible and transparent business practices: the Hybrid AI Forecast Model, the Ethics-First Predictive Model, and the Transparent Multi-Layered Ensemble Model.

Hybrid AI Forecast Model: Integrating Human Judgment with Machine Learning

The Hybrid AI Forecast Model leverages the best of both worlds: the computational power of machine learning algorithms and the nuanced insights of human financial analysts. This model addresses one of the primary concerns in AI financial forecasting—ensuring that human intuition and experience remain part of the decision-making process.

1. Model Overview and Methodology

The Hybrid AI Forecast Model combines traditional statistical forecasting techniques with advanced machine learning algorithms. The model operates in two main phases: an initial machine learning-driven prediction phase and a human validation and adjustment phase. In the first phase, the AI component uses large datasets, such as historical financial data, macroeconomic indicators, and real-time market conditions, to generate initial forecasts. These forecasts are based on algorithms like Long Short-Term Memory (LSTM) networks, which excel at capturing complex time-series patterns.

Once the AI generates predictions, human financial experts review the forecasts. They consider factors that may not be adequately captured by AI, such as geopolitical risks, regulatory changes, or shifts in consumer behavior. Analysts can adjust the forecasts based on their domain expertise, creating a final, integrated prediction that reflects both data-driven insights and human judgment.

2. Ethical Considerations and Implementation

The Hybrid AI Forecast Model emphasizes transparency and accountability. Human analysts are required to document any adjustments they make to the AI-generated forecasts, explaining the rationale behind their changes. This documentation serves as a valuable record for governance and ensures that human biases are minimized and openly acknowledged. Additionally, the model employs explainable AI (XAI) techniques to provide insights into the AI component's decision-making process, fostering trust and understanding among stakeholders.

3. Benefits and Strategic Advantages

By combining AI and human expertise, this model mitigates the risks associated with over-reliance on either approach. The machine learning component ensures forecasts are data-driven and scalable, while human oversight introduces flexibility and contextual awareness. Businesses using this model benefit from increased forecast accuracy, faster decision-making, and a more holistic understanding of financial risks.

4. Challenges and Limitations

Implementing a Hybrid AI Forecast Model requires significant investment in both technology and human capital. Companies must train financial analysts to understand and work alongside AI systems effectively. Additionally, there is a risk that human biases may still influence the final forecasts, despite efforts to maintain objectivity.

Ethics-First Predictive Model: Prioritizing Fairness, Transparency, and Accountability

The Ethics-First Predictive Model is designed with ethical principles as a core component. This model ensures that AI-driven financial forecasts are fair, transparent, and accountable, addressing concerns about algorithmic bias and decision-making opacity in the financial sector.

1. Model Overview and Methodology

The Ethics-First Predictive Model employs a multi-step approach to ensure ethical forecasting. First, the model uses fairness-aware algorithms that are trained to minimize biases across different demographic groups or market segments. For instance, in scenarios where AI forecasts are used for consumer lending or investment risk assessments, the model includes constraints that prevent discrimination based on gender, ethnicity, or socioeconomic status.

Second, the model incorporates a robust audit trail. Every forecast generated by the AI is accompanied by a detailed explanation of the underlying factors that influenced the prediction. This includes data sources, key variables, and the model's internal decision-making logic. Furthermore, an independent ethics review board regularly audits the AI system, evaluating its performance and fairness.

2. Ethical Considerations and Implementation

A key feature of the Ethics-First Predictive Model is its commitment to transparency. Businesses that adopt this model must publish periodic reports detailing the model's impact on different stakeholder groups. This open communication fosters trust with investors, customers, and regulators. Additionally, the model includes mechanisms for stakeholder feedback, allowing external parties to raise concerns about potential biases or inaccuracies.

3. Benefits and Strategic Advantages

The Ethics-First Predictive Model enhances corporate social responsibility and compliance with emerging AI regulations. By prioritizing fairness and accountability, companies can differentiate themselves as ethical leaders in the market. This model also helps mitigate legal risks, as it is designed to comply with global regulations, such as the European Union's General Data Protection Regulation (GDPR) and the proposed AI Act.

From a financial perspective, ethical forecasting can also improve brand reputation and attract socially conscious investors. Moreover, the model's emphasis on transparency reduces the risk of unexpected financial outcomes, as stakeholders have a clear understanding of how forecasts are generated.

4. Challenges and Limitations

Despite its advantages, the Ethics-First Predictive Model is complex and resource-intensive. Ensuring fairness in AI models often requires re-engineering data pipelines and implementing sophisticated monitoring systems. Additionally, the model's emphasis on transparency may slow down the forecasting process, as generating detailed audit trails and reports takes time.

Transparent Multi-Layered Ensemble Model: A Data-Driven Approach with Enhanced Oversight

The Transparent Multi-Layered Ensemble Model leverages the power of ensemble learning to generate highly accurate financial forecasts while maintaining a strong focus on transparency and interpretability. Ensemble learning combines predictions from multiple AI models to improve overall performance and reduce the risk of errors.

1. Model Overview and Methodology

This model integrates several different types of forecasting algorithms, such as decision trees, neural networks, and Bayesian models. By aggregating predictions from multiple models, the ensemble approach reduces the risk of overfitting and enhances forecast reliability. The model is structured into three key layers:

- Layer 1: Data Preprocessing and Integrity Checks

The first layer focuses on data quality. It employs AI-driven tools to clean and preprocess data, identifying and correcting any inconsistencies. This layer ensures that only high-quality, unbiased data is used for forecasting, which is crucial for accurate predictions.

- Layer 2: Model Diversity and Aggregation

The second layer comprises multiple AI models, each trained on different subsets of the data. By introducing diversity in the models, the ensemble approach mitigates the risk of any single model's weaknesses impacting the final forecast. Techniques like weighted averaging or voting mechanisms are used to combine the predictions in a balanced way.

- Layer 3: Explainability and Oversight

The third layer focuses on explainability and oversight. Advanced interpretability techniques, such as Shapley values and Local Interpretable Model-agnostic Explanations (LIME), are used to provide detailed insights into how each model contributes to the final forecast. Additionally, this layer includes human oversight committees that review the forecasts and approve them before they are disseminated.

2. Ethical Considerations and Implementation

The Transparent Multi-Layered Ensemble Model ensures that AI-driven forecasts are interpretable and easy to audit. Businesses must establish governance frameworks that define who is responsible for monitoring the model's performance and addressing any ethical concerns. The model also includes built-in alerts that notify stakeholders if significant deviations or biases are detected in the forecasts.

3. Benefits and Strategic Advantages

This model excels in scenarios where accuracy and transparency are equally important. It provides businesses with robust, data-driven forecasts while ensuring that stakeholders understand how decisions are made. By offering a comprehensive view of financial trends, the ensemble approach enables more confident strategic planning and risk management. The model's transparency features also facilitate compliance with regulatory requirements, reducing the risk of fines and reputational damage.

From a strategic perspective, the model's emphasis on diversity and interpretability allows businesses to adapt quickly to changing market conditions. By understanding the factors driving AI forecasts, decision-makers can respond proactively to emerging risks and opportunities.

4. Challenges and Limitations

The Transparent Multi-Layered Ensemble Model is computationally intensive and requires substantial infrastructure. Companies must invest in high-performance computing resources and data storage solutions to support the model. Additionally, the complexity of managing multiple AI models can be daunting, necessitating specialized expertise in AI and data science.

Each of the three AI-driven forecasting models presented in this chapter offers unique advantages and ethical considerations. The Hybrid AI Forecast Model is ideal for organizations seeking a balanced approach that integrates human expertise with machine learning. The Ethics-First Predictive Model is perfect for companies prioritizing fairness, transparency, and accountability in their financial practices. Meanwhile, the Transparent Multi-Layered Ensemble Model is best suited for businesses that require high accuracy and interpretability in their forecasts.

Ultimately, the choice of model depends on a company's strategic objectives, ethical commitments, and regulatory environment. By adopting one of these models, businesses can harness the power of AI for financial forecasting while maintaining responsible and transparent practices. The future of financial forecasting lies in models that are not only data-driven but also ethically and strategically sound.

Model	Key Features	Ethical Considerations	Benefits	Challenges
Hybrid AI Forecast Model	- Combines machine learning and human judgment	- Human oversight may introduce bias	- Balances data-driven accuracy with human insights	- High investment in technology and human training needed
	- AI-driven prediction followed by human adjustment	- Requires documentation of human adjustments	- Scalable and adaptable forecasting	- Potential for subjective human influence
	- Uses LSTM networks and explainable AI	- Promotes transparency and accountability	- Improved trust and holistic risk management	- Complex integration of AI and human processes
Ethics-First Predictive Model	- Fairness-aware algorithms to minimize bias	- Ongoing fairness audits and independent reviews	- Strong compliance with ethical and regulatory standards	- Resource-intensive to implement and maintain
	- Robust audit trail and explainability	- Transparency and regular public reporting	- Enhanced corporate social responsibility	- Slower forecasting due to transparency requirements

	- Independent ethics review board	- Requires stakeholder feedback mechanisms	- Attracts socially conscious investors	- Complex data re-engineering to prevent bias
Transparent Multi-Layered Ensemble Model	- Ensemble learning using multiple AI models	- Governance frameworks for accountability	- High accuracy and reduced risk of errors	- Computationally intensive and infrastructure-heavy
	- Data preprocessing layer ensures high data quality	- Built-in alerts for bias and significant deviations	- Detailed insights for confident strategic planning	- Requires specialized AI and data science expertise
	- Interpretability techniques like Shapley values, LIME	- Emphasis on explainability for all forecasts	- Facilitates regulatory compliance and proactive risk management	- Managing multiple models is complex and demanding

CHAPTER 5: THE FUTURE IS NOW – INTEGRATING AI INTO LONG-TERM STRATEGIC PLANNING

In an era where rapid technological evolution shapes the very fabric of industries, one truth has become inescapable: artificial intelligence (AI) is no longer just an optional tool or a distant vision for businesses—it is a present force, reshaping the methodologies of strategic planning. In Chapter 5, we embark on a deep dive into how integrating AI into long-term strategic planning can unlock unprecedented potential for businesses, streamline complex decision-making, and offer a competitive edge that is essential for navigating the 21st century.

The Paradigm Shift in Strategic Planning

For decades, long-term strategic planning has been synonymous with rigorous analysis, historical data scrutiny, and forecasts based on economic, market, and behavioral trends. However, as these factors became increasingly intricate and interconnected, even the most sophisticated human-led processes struggled to keep up. Enter AI: a technological powerhouse capable of processing colossal datasets, identifying hidden patterns, and generating predictive models that enhance human intuition and expertise.

Imagine planning a five-year business strategy in a volatile global market. The usual approach would involve gathering data from disparate sources, employing consultants, and basing projections on past trends with educated guesses about future shifts. Now, picture an AI system capable of analyzing real-time data, simulating thousands of potential future scenarios, and optimizing strategies that adapt dynamically as new information flows in. This is the new landscape of strategic planning—an adaptive, data-driven approach where AI isn't just a supplement but a co-pilot.

Transformative Benefits of AI in Strategic Planning

What makes AI so transformative for strategic planning? Let's delve into its core advantages:

1. Enhanced Predictive Analysis: Traditional forecasting models often grapple with the limitations of linearity and static data sets. AI, on the other hand, uses machine learning algorithms to refine its predictions continuously. For instance, businesses in the energy sector can leverage AI to analyze years of meteorological data, energy consumption trends,

and geopolitical events, producing more accurate long-term supply and demand forecasts. This reduces the risk of costly missteps and enables companies to position themselves more strategically.

2. Agility and Adaptability: One of the most profound benefits of AI is its ability to adapt. Unlike human strategists bound by decision inertia, AI systems can process new data almost instantaneously and recommend course corrections. This agility is particularly valuable in industries prone to disruption. Picture a multinational company navigating international trade policy changes or sudden supply chain disruptions. AI can rapidly synthesize the implications, propose contingencies, and inform decision-makers on the best path forward, turning potential crises into opportunities for growth.

3. Unbiased Decision-Making: Humans are inherently susceptible to cognitive biases—anchoring, overconfidence, and the status quo bias, to name a few. These biases can seep into long-term strategic planning, clouding judgment and leading to suboptimal outcomes. AI, however, approaches data analytically, free from emotional or experiential biases. While it's essential to note that AI can reflect biases present in training data, strategic integration ensures that these are identified and minimized, enhancing objectivity.

4. Cost Efficiency: Integrating AI into strategic planning might seem like a hefty investment initially, but it translates to long-term cost savings. Automating complex analyses reduces the need for extensive human resources and consultancy fees. Moreover, AI's predictive accuracy can preempt costly miscalculations, safeguarding both financial health and business reputation.

Practical Applications Across Industries

The integration of AI into strategic planning isn't an abstract concept; it's already being executed across industries with remarkable results. Let's look at some practical applications that illustrate this transformation:

- Retail and Supply Chain Management: Retail giants employ AI to predict demand, optimize inventory, and streamline logistics. Advanced AI models factor in variables like regional weather forecasts, consumer behavior insights, and supplier data to ensure the right products are available at the right time. For instance, an AI-driven strategic plan can recommend stocking more snow gear in cities expecting colder winters or more swimwear during anticipated warm summers.

- Finance and Investment Strategy: Financial institutions leverage AI for portfolio management and investment strategy. Traditional fund managers analyze past performances and economic indicators, but AI can look further—identifying correlations hidden in historical, real-time, and alternative datasets (such as social media sentiment and consumer trends). The result? Portfolios that can adapt to market swings, improving returns and reducing exposure to volatility.

- Healthcare: In the complex world of healthcare, AI aids in strategic planning for both providers and pharmaceutical companies. Machine learning algorithms help hospitals predict patient admission rates and allocate resources efficiently, while pharmaceutical firms use AI to optimize drug development timelines, strategically targeting research investments for maximum potential.

Challenges and Considerations

Despite its immense potential, integrating AI into strategic planning comes with its challenges. Here are some key considerations that businesses must address:

1. Data Quality and Integration: AI is only as powerful as the data it processes. Inconsistent, outdated, or biased data can lead to flawed insights. Businesses must invest in robust data collection and integration systems to harness the true power of AI.

2. Human Oversight: While AI can perform analyses far beyond human capability, it cannot replace the intuition, creativity, and ethical reasoning of human strategists. AI should be seen as a partner—augmenting human decision-making, not replacing it. A successful integration relies on a symbiotic relationship where AI and human expertise complement each other.

3. Ethical and Compliance Issues: The use of AI in long-term strategic planning must align with ethical standards and regulatory requirements. Data privacy concerns, AI's potential biases, and transparency in decision-making are non-negotiable factors that organizations must proactively manage. Establishing governance frameworks for AI use ensures that the technology serves not only the company's interests but broader societal values as well.

Steps to Seamless AI Integration

So, how can a business begin its journey of integrating AI into its strategic planning framework? Here's a roadmap:

1. Define Strategic Objectives Clearly: Before deploying AI, businesses must outline clear goals. Are they seeking to improve forecasting accuracy, reduce risks, or enhance operational efficiency? A well-defined objective will guide AI system selection and implementation.

2. Invest in the Right Tools and Expertise: The market is flooded with AI solutions, but not all are suitable for strategic planning. Companies should assess tools that align with their needs, seeking solutions capable of analyzing multidimensional datasets and generating actionable insights. Equally important is investing in talent—AI specialists who understand both the technical aspects and business strategy are invaluable.

3. Foster a Culture of Data Literacy: For AI integration to be effective, organizations must ensure that their teams are comfortable with data-driven insights. This doesn't mean

everyone needs to be a data scientist, but stakeholders should understand the basics of how AI works and what its recommendations mean. Training programs and workshops can bridge this gap.

4. Start Small and Scale Up: It can be tempting to overhaul the entire strategic process with AI from the get-go, but starting with pilot programs is more effective. Small-scale projects allow businesses to test AI systems, learn from implementation challenges, and refine processes before a broader rollout.

Interactive Thought Experiment

Let's pause for a moment and consider this scenario: You are the CEO of a global consumer electronics company. Your strategic plan involves expanding into new markets in Asia and Europe. You have access to traditional data, such as market trends and economic forecasts, but you decide to integrate AI for deeper insights.

Now, imagine an AI-driven dashboard that displays not only current market data but also simulations of consumer behavior shifts in response to economic events, competitor actions, and potential supply chain disruptions. You notice that while market projections are optimistic for Asia, an AI-generated scenario indicates a looming risk in the supply chain due to potential regulatory changes in semiconductor exports.

How would you use this information? Would you adjust your timeline, diversify suppliers, or double down on research and development to develop proprietary technology? This level of insight transforms your role from a reactive strategist to a proactive, informed leader who anticipates challenges and seizes opportunities.

The Future Calls for Bold Steps

As we stand at the intersection of technological innovation and strategic ambition, integrating AI into long-term strategic planning is no longer a futuristic aspiration—it is a present necessity. The businesses that embrace AI as a core component of their planning will not only weather the uncertainties of the future but will thrive in them. They will be the ones redefining industry standards, reshaping markets, and leading with agility and foresight.

Are we ready to step into this AI-powered future? The potential is immense, but it requires a commitment to change, investment in technology, and a culture that values data-driven decisions. The future isn't waiting for tomorrow—it is unfolding right now. Those who grasp it will lead; those who don't risk being left behind.

What are your thoughts? Can your organization or industry benefit from AI's transformative potential in long-term strategic planning? How prepared are we collectively to embrace this shift?

Future Challenges of AI Integration in Strategic Planning: Opportunities and Risks for Businesses

As businesses navigate the integration of artificial intelligence (AI) into their strategic planning, several future challenges emerge. While the promise of AI brings immense potential for transformation and growth, it also comes with significant risks and complexities. Companies that can skillfully manage these will find themselves at the forefront of their industries. This section will delve into the most critical future challenges posed by AI in strategic planning, exploring both opportunities and the inherent risks they entail.

1. Data Management and Quality

The Challenge: The foundation of effective AI integration lies in high-quality data. For AI models to yield reliable insights, businesses must ensure their data is comprehensive, clean, and current. However, data collection, storage, and maintenance present challenges. Fragmented data sources, outdated information, and inconsistencies can lead to flawed AI outputs. Moreover, with the exponential growth of data, managing its sheer volume and variety becomes increasingly complex.

Opportunity: Companies that invest in robust data governance frameworks can harness AI to turn data into a strategic asset. High-quality data allows for deeper insights, leading to more accurate forecasts, better risk assessments, and more effective decision-making. Organizations that excel in data management can use AI to create predictive models that improve over time, allowing them to anticipate market trends and consumer needs with increasing precision.

Risk: Poor data quality can result in misleading AI-generated insights. Decisions based on inaccurate data can lead to costly errors, missed opportunities, and strategic missteps. For instance, an AI system that relies on biased or incomplete data might suggest entering a market where actual conditions are far less favorable than predicted. Furthermore, maintaining data quality comes with significant costs and requires a dedicated infrastructure and skilled personnel.

2. Ethical and Regulatory Concerns

The Challenge: AI's use in strategic planning raises profound ethical and regulatory questions. Concerns about data privacy, transparency in AI algorithms, and potential biases are at the forefront. Regulations such as the General Data Protection Regulation (GDPR) in the European Union already impose strict rules on data handling, and more such regulations are expected to emerge worldwide.

Opportunity: Companies that proactively adopt ethical AI practices and build transparent models can position themselves as leaders in corporate responsibility. Implementing rigorous ethical guidelines and compliance frameworks not only helps meet current regulations but also prepares businesses for future legal developments. This approach builds trust with customers and stakeholders, enhancing brand reputation and customer loyalty.

Risk: Non-compliance with data regulations can lead to severe financial penalties and reputational damage. Additionally, the opacity of certain AI models, known as "black box" AI, poses risks as decision-makers might struggle to understand how conclusions are reached. This lack of transparency can be problematic if decisions are called into question by regulatory bodies or the public. Businesses that fail to address these ethical concerns may face backlash, reduced consumer trust, and potential boycotts.

3. Bias and Fairness

The Challenge: Bias in AI is an ongoing issue that poses significant challenges for strategic planning. AI models learn from historical data, and if that data contains biases, the models will replicate and potentially amplify them. This can result in unfair outcomes that may affect hiring practices, marketing strategies, or investment decisions.

Opportunity: Addressing AI bias can become a competitive advantage. Companies that develop AI models with fairness and inclusivity in mind can avoid negative public relations incidents and foster a more diverse and innovative business environment. Moreover, inclusive AI can help businesses better understand and serve a wider range of customers, leading to increased market share.

Risk: Biased AI can lead to decisions that discriminate against certain groups or propagate systemic inequalities, opening businesses to potential legal action and reputational damage. For example, an AI tool that unintentionally favors candidates from specific backgrounds in hiring decisions can result in public outcry and possible lawsuits. The challenge of bias goes beyond ethics—it impacts a company's ability to make fair and balanced decisions, thus undermining strategic integrity.

4. Workforce Implications

The Challenge: The integration of AI into strategic planning changes the nature of work, impacting job roles, skills requirements, and employment levels. As AI takes over tasks traditionally handled by human strategists, concerns about job displacement and the future of the workforce grow.

Opportunity: AI can be leveraged to augment human capabilities rather than replace them. By automating routine and repetitive tasks, businesses can free up human employees to focus on higher-value activities such as creative problem-solving, strategic thinking, and interpersonal relationship management. This shift can lead to increased productivity and innovation. Companies that invest in upskilling their workforce to work alongside AI will not only ease the transition but also enhance their employees' ability to use AI tools effectively.

Risk: Without proper workforce management, the integration of AI can lead to significant job losses and reduced morale among employees. Resistance to change can stifle AI adoption, making it difficult for businesses to realize the full potential of their investments. Additionally, there is the risk of creating a workforce skills gap, where employees are ill-equipped to work with advanced AI systems. Companies failing to address these concerns may face high turnover rates and struggle to attract new talent.

5. Dependence on Technology Providers

The Challenge: The use of advanced AI solutions often requires partnerships with specialized technology providers. This dependency can be risky if a company becomes too reliant on a single provider, which may lead to issues related to vendor lock-in, limited flexibility, and potential disruptions if the provider encounters problems or changes its business strategy.

Opportunity: Strategic alliances with technology providers can enable businesses to access cutting-edge AI tools and capabilities without developing these technologies in-house. By diversifying partnerships and maintaining strong vendor management practices, companies can leverage the expertise of various providers to enhance their strategic planning processes.

Risk: Relying heavily on third-party providers increases a company's exposure to potential data security risks, intellectual property issues, and service interruptions. If a provider goes out of business or faces a major cybersecurity breach, client companies may suffer significant operational setbacks. To mitigate this, businesses need to prioritize vendor risk assessments and develop contingency plans to maintain continuity.

6. Integration Complexity

The Challenge: Integrating AI into long-term strategic planning requires the seamless blending of new technology with existing processes and systems. This integration is often complex, involving cross-functional collaboration and substantial changes to traditional business workflows.

Opportunity: Companies that successfully integrate AI can build more efficient, responsive, and data-driven strategic processes. AI systems can be embedded in various departments, creating interconnected networks where strategic insights are shared and utilized across the organization. This leads to more cohesive and aligned business strategies that can respond rapidly to changes in the market.

Risk: Integration challenges can lead to disruptions in existing workflows and create friction between teams. Resistance to adopting new technologies can stall projects and reduce employee engagement. Additionally, integrating AI requires significant investment in infrastructure and training, which may be prohibitive for smaller firms. The failure to integrate AI effectively can lead to fragmented data systems and siloed decision-making, diminishing the potential benefits of AI.

7. Cybersecurity Threats

The Challenge: With AI-driven strategic planning relying heavily on digital infrastructure, cybersecurity becomes an essential concern. The more sophisticated AI systems become, the more attractive they are as targets for cyberattacks. AI models themselves can be manipulated through data poisoning or adversarial attacks, where malicious actors introduce subtle changes to input data to alter the system's output.

Opportunity: Companies that prioritize cybersecurity as part of their AI strategy can set themselves apart as secure and reliable partners. AI can also be used defensively to strengthen security measures, identifying and responding to threats faster than traditional methods. This dual role of AI—as both a tool for strategic planning and a means to bolster cybersecurity—can enhance a company's resilience.

Risk: If cybersecurity is neglected, businesses expose themselves to potential data breaches, intellectual property theft, and operational disruptions. The consequences of a successful cyberattack can be severe, resulting in loss of sensitive information, regulatory penalties, and significant damage to a company's reputation. The rapid evolution of cyber threats means that staying one step ahead requires constant vigilance and investment.

8. Scalability and Continuous Improvement

The Challenge: As businesses grow, their needs and strategic objectives evolve. AI models and strategies must scale accordingly. However, scaling AI involves more than increasing processing power; it requires ongoing training, model updates, and ensuring that AI systems continue to align with strategic goals as these shift over time.

Opportunity: Businesses that build AI frameworks capable of scaling can leverage technology to support expansion into new markets, product launches, and other strategic initiatives. AI's ability to learn and adapt means that it can improve its performance over time, providing continuously optimized recommendations and strategies.

Risk: Scaling AI is not without its hurdles. Companies may encounter issues related to maintaining the quality of data inputs and ensuring consistency across different business units or regions. The complexity of scaling can also strain IT and human resources, requiring continual updates to systems, retraining of models, and adaptation of business practices. If scaling is not managed effectively, companies risk operational inefficiencies and strategic misalignment.

Balancing the AI Equation

The integration of AI into long-term strategic planning presents businesses with a dynamic landscape of opportunities and risks. The future success of AI adoption depends on how well companies can balance the powerful advantages of AI—such as enhanced predictive analysis, greater agility, and cost savings—against the challenges of data quality, ethical considerations, workforce impacts, and cybersecurity.

To navigate these waters, businesses must adopt a forward-thinking approach. This includes committing to continuous improvement, fostering collaboration between AI specialists and human strategists, and investing in both technology and people. Moreover, companies need to stay informed about regulatory developments and ensure their practices align with evolving ethical and compliance standards.

Businesses that can manage the complexities of AI integration will not only position themselves to thrive in a competitive landscape but will also contribute to shaping an ethical, inclusive, and forward-thinking industry standard. The future of strategic planning is already here; now, it's up to leaders to navigate it with foresight, adaptability, and responsibility.

APPENDICES

Appendix A: Key AI Tools and Platforms for Business Leaders

In the evolving world of finance, economics, and business strategy, the integration of AI has become a pivotal aspect of remaining competitive and adaptive. Business leaders must familiarize themselves with a range of AI tools that can enhance decision-making, drive efficiency, and unlock new opportunities. This appendix provides an overview of some of the most impactful AI tools and platforms available today. These tools have been selected for their relevance, usability, and potential to transform business processes.

1. Data Analysis and Predictive Modeling Platforms

- IBM Watson Studio: A powerful AI platform that allows businesses to build, train, and deploy machine learning models. Watson Studio supports a collaborative environment where data scientists and business analysts can work together to refine data models, optimize algorithms, and predict outcomes. Its capabilities in natural language processing (NLP) and deep learning make it suitable for deriving insights from unstructured data.

- Microsoft Azure Machine Learning: Known for its versatility and integration capabilities with existing enterprise systems, this platform offers a suite of tools for developing predictive models. It supports automated machine learning (AutoML), enabling non-technical users to create models with minimal coding. For businesses seeking scalability and robust data integration, Azure's seamless connection with Microsoft products provides an added advantage.

2. Customer Experience and Personalization Tools

- Salesforce Einstein: Embedded within the Salesforce ecosystem, Einstein provides advanced analytics and AI-driven insights that enhance customer engagement. Through predictive analysis and sentiment tracking, businesses can anticipate customer needs and personalize experiences at scale. The tool's ease of use and intuitive dashboards make it accessible for teams looking to leverage data-driven marketing strategies.

- HubSpot's AI-Powered CRM: HubSpot has incorporated AI to offer features like automated lead scoring, personalized content recommendations, and workflow optimization. This tool is especially beneficial for small to mid-sized businesses looking to improve customer relations and automate repetitive tasks.

3. Natural Language Processing (NLP) and Automation Tools

- OpenAI's GPT Series: The Generative Pre-trained Transformer (GPT) models, such as GPT-4, have been transformative for content generation, customer service automation, and real-time data analysis. Businesses use these models to develop chatbots, automate report generation, and even generate code. The versatility of OpenAI's platform allows firms to tailor its usage to their specific needs, whether that be streamlining communication or synthesizing large data sets.

- Dialogflow by Google: An NLP platform designed for building conversational interfaces, Dialogflow powers chatbots and voice assistants. With its intuitive interface and robust machine learning backend, businesses can create customer support bots, virtual assistants, and interactive service platforms. The tool integrates well with various communication channels such as web, mobile apps, and smart home devices.

4. Business Intelligence (BI) Tools

- Tableau: Tableau remains a leader in the data visualization space, providing businesses with the ability to transform complex data into clear, actionable dashboards. The tool's AI-enhanced features like "Ask Data" allow users to input natural language questions and receive visual answers. Tableau's ease of integration with other data sources makes it essential for leaders aiming to foster data-driven cultures.

- Power BI by Microsoft: Power BI combines user-friendly data visualization capabilities with AI-powered analytics. It supports seamless data connections and offers advanced AI features like cognitive services integration, enabling leaders to implement complex analytics without extensive coding knowledge. The platform is ideal for creating real-time reports and interactive visual representations that support strategic decisions.

5. AI-Powered Strategic Management and Forecasting Tools

- Alteryx: For data preparation and advanced analytics, Alteryx simplifies complex data workflows. Its AI-powered predictive modeling features allow teams to experiment with different business scenarios and understand their potential outcomes. This tool is especially effective in strategic decision-making, helping leaders forecast sales, manage supply chains, and optimize operations.

- SAP Leonardo: Integrating AI, machine learning, and blockchain technology, SAP Leonardo is designed to bring intelligent data insights to traditional business functions. From supply chain management to customer behavior analysis, SAP Leonardo enables leaders to draw from real-time data streams and respond proactively to changing market dynamics.

6. AI Ethics and Governance Tools

- Ethical AI Platforms by Deloitte: Addressing the growing concerns about bias and ethical transparency in AI, platforms such as Deloitte's Ethical AI tools help organizations audit their AI models for fairness and accountability. These platforms provide diagnostic capabilities that ensure AI deployment aligns with regulatory standards and corporate responsibility goals.

- AI Explainability 360 by IBM: As businesses integrate AI into critical operations, the demand for transparent AI models has surged. IBM's AI Explainability 360 toolkit assists teams in understanding, trusting, and managing AI models by offering a range of interpretability algorithms. This is especially valuable for highly regulated industries like finance and healthcare.

Appendix B: Case Studies and Success Stories – Lessons from Industry Pioneers

To illustrate the practical benefits and applications of AI-powered strategies, this appendix delves into real-world case studies. These examples underscore how businesses across various sectors have harnessed AI to drive growth, innovate, and gain a competitive edge.

1. Retail Industry: Walmart's Predictive Analytics Revolution

Walmart, one of the world's largest retail chains, has long been a pioneer in the adoption of data analytics to optimize its operations. Faced with the challenge of managing vast inventories across thousands of stores, Walmart integrated predictive analytics powered by machine learning algorithms to streamline supply chain management. By analyzing real-time purchasing data, weather patterns, and regional trends, Walmart accurately forecasted product demand and minimized overstock and stockouts.

Lesson Learned: The strategic application of predictive analytics can significantly enhance operational efficiency, reduce costs, and improve customer satisfaction. Business leaders should consider the value of predictive modeling in forecasting trends and aligning supply with demand.

2. Finance Sector: JPMorgan Chase's COiN Platform

JPMorgan Chase's Contract Intelligence (COiN) platform is a prime example of how AI can transform traditionally manual, time-intensive processes. COiN uses natural language processing to review and interpret complex legal documents. What once required up to 360,000 hours of manpower annually now takes seconds, with the system accurately extracting essential data from millions of documents.

Lesson Learned: Automating routine processes with AI not only reduces operational costs but also reallocates human talent to higher-value tasks. Leaders in highly regulated sectors can leverage AI to manage data-heavy workflows more efficiently and with reduced risk.

3. Healthcare: Mayo Clinic's AI-Enhanced Diagnostics

The Mayo Clinic has integrated AI into its diagnostic protocols to improve accuracy and patient outcomes. By employing deep learning algorithms, the clinic has enhanced its ability to detect early signs of disease from radiology scans and patient data. In one notable study, AI was used to identify early-stage breast cancer with accuracy rates exceeding those of experienced radiologists.

Lesson Learned: The integration of AI in medical diagnostics demonstrates that strategic AI deployment can lead to breakthroughs in quality and service delivery. Business leaders in healthcare should view AI not just as a tool for enhancing operational efficiency but as a pathway to delivering life-changing results.

4. E-commerce: Amazon's Personalization Engine

Amazon's recommendation engine, powered by advanced machine learning algorithms, has been central to its success. The company's AI models analyze a vast array of customer data points—including purchase history, browsing behavior, and ratings—to deliver personalized product recommendations. This targeted approach has contributed to a significant portion of Amazon's revenue, showcasing the power of personalized marketing.

Lesson Learned: Personalization is key in retaining customers and driving sales. AI tools that can analyze user behavior and adapt to changing preferences can foster customer loyalty and expand market share. Leaders should prioritize customer-centric strategies powered by data analytics to stay competitive.

5. Manufacturing: General Electric (GE) and Predictive Maintenance

GE has been a trailblazer in adopting AI to transform its manufacturing processes through predictive maintenance. Leveraging sensors and AI analytics on its machinery, GE has been able to predict failures before they occur, scheduling maintenance at optimal times to avoid disruptions. This proactive approach has reduced downtime, enhanced productivity, and extended the life of its equipment.

Lesson Learned: Predictive maintenance is an area where AI can have immediate and measurable effects. Leaders in industries reliant on equipment should explore AI-driven solutions that enhance operational reliability and reduce costs through smarter maintenance strategies.

6. Energy Sector: Shell's AI-Driven Efficiency

Shell has utilized AI to optimize its exploration and drilling operations. The company partnered with analytics firms to develop machine learning models that analyze seismic data, helping geologists identify viable drilling locations with greater accuracy.

Additionally, Shell's predictive AI systems monitor equipment and operational parameters, flagging potential issues before they escalate.

Lesson Learned: The energy sector demonstrates how AI can intersect with complex engineering and environmental data to make better business decisions. For leaders in resource-intensive industries, adopting AI can lead to safer, more efficient, and more sustainable operations.

7. Financial Services: Ant Group's AI for Risk Management

Ant Group, the financial affiliate of Alibaba, has effectively implemented AI to assess credit risks and streamline loan approvals. By harnessing AI algorithms that analyze both structured and unstructured data, the company can quickly evaluate borrower credibility and predict loan performance. This has enabled faster lending processes and broadened access to financial services for individuals and small businesses.

Lesson Learned: AI in financial services can democratize access and improve decision-making accuracy. Business leaders should view AI not just as a tool for profit but as a means of creating more inclusive financial ecosystems.

8. Transportation: Uber's Real-Time Route Optimization

Uber has revolutionized urban transportation through its use of AI. The company's machine learning algorithms dynamically optimize routes based on real-time traffic data, driver availability, and passenger locations. This has reduced wait times for customers and improved the overall efficiency of its service.

Lesson Learned: Real-time data analysis and algorithmic optimization are invaluable in service industries where speed and efficiency are critical. Leaders should seek ways to integrate real-time analytics into their logistics and customer service operations to improve responsiveness and user satisfaction.

The case studies presented demonstrate that AI is not just an optional upgrade but a transformative element that redefines industries. From healthcare and retail to finance and manufacturing, the ability of AI to extract value from data and automate complex tasks allows businesses to innovate and grow. These appendices aim to provide a comprehensive roadmap for leaders seeking to understand the strategic deployment of AI and to learn from pioneers who have successfully navigated the journey.

Appendix C: Glossary of AI Terms for Non-Technical Readers

Understanding artificial intelligence (AI) can be challenging due to the technical jargon often used in discussions. This glossary demystifies key terms, ensuring that business leaders and professionals without technical backgrounds can grasp the essentials of AI and its applications.

A. Foundational AI Terms

- Artificial Intelligence (AI): The field of computer science focused on creating systems capable of performing tasks that typically require human intelligence, such as learning, reasoning, and problem-solving.

- Machine Learning (ML): A subset of AI that enables systems to learn from data and improve performance over time without being explicitly programmed. ML algorithms build models based on input data and use them to make predictions or decisions.

- Deep Learning: A more advanced subset of machine learning involving neural networks with multiple layers (deep neural networks). It mimics the human brain's functioning to recognize patterns and make decisions with a high degree of accuracy.

- Neural Network: A series of algorithms modeled after the human brain's structure, designed to recognize patterns by interpreting sensory data. Used widely in image recognition, language translation, and more.

- Algorithm: A set of rules or instructions that a computer follows to perform a task or solve a problem. In AI, algorithms underpin how models learn from data and make predictions.

B. Data and Model-Related Terms

- Training Data: A dataset used to train an AI model. The model learns to recognize patterns and relationships in this data, forming the basis for making predictions.

- Test Data: Data that is used to evaluate the performance and accuracy of a trained AI model. It ensures the model can generalize and perform well on unseen data.

- Overfitting: A scenario where an AI model learns the training data too well, including noise and details that do not generalize to new data. This reduces its predictive performance on real-world data.

- Feature: An individual measurable property or characteristic of a phenomenon being observed. For instance, in customer analysis, features might include age, purchase history, or location.

- Label: The outcome or target variable used in supervised learning, which the model aims to predict. For example, in spam detection, emails are labeled as either "spam" or "not spam."

C. Model Performance and Types

- Supervised Learning: A type of machine learning where the model is trained on labeled data, meaning the input and the correct output are provided. It's used in applications like email classification and fraud detection.

- Unsupervised Learning: The AI model learns from unlabeled data and identifies hidden patterns or intrinsic structures without specific guidance. Clustering and association tasks, such as market segmentation, fall into this category.

- Reinforcement Learning: A type of learning where an agent interacts with its environment and learns by receiving rewards or penalties. This approach is popular in robotics, game-playing AI, and autonomous systems.

- Accuracy: A measure of how often an AI model correctly predicts outcomes. It is calculated as the ratio of correct predictions to total predictions made.

- Bias: Systematic errors that occur when an AI model's predictions are consistently skewed due to imbalanced training data or flawed model design. Bias can result in unfair or misleading outcomes.

- Precision and Recall: Metrics used to evaluate the performance of a classification model. Precision measures the accuracy of positive predictions, while recall assesses the model's ability to identify all relevant instances.

D. Advanced Concepts and Practical Applications

- Natural Language Processing (NLP): A branch of AI that enables computers to understand, interpret, and generate human language. It's used in chatbots, sentiment analysis, and language translation tools.

- Computer Vision: A field of AI that trains computers to interpret and process visual information from the world, similar to human vision. Applications include facial recognition, image analysis, and autonomous vehicles.

- Robotic Process Automation (RPA): The use of software robots to automate highly repetitive, rule-based tasks traditionally performed by humans, such as data entry and form processing.

- Cognitive Computing: Systems that mimic human thought processes to enhance decision-making. These include AI models that can handle complex analyses and reason like humans.

- Explainability: The degree to which the decision-making process of an AI system can be understood by humans. It is essential for building trust, particularly in sensitive sectors like finance and healthcare.

Appendix D: Resources for Continued Learning and Development in AI

The dynamic nature of AI means that staying informed and up-to-date is crucial for business leaders. This appendix outlines recommended resources that cater to different learning preferences, from online courses and podcasts to influential publications and AI communities.

1. Online Courses and Certifications

- Coursera – Machine Learning by Stanford University: Taught by AI expert Andrew Ng, this foundational course introduces core concepts in machine learning and data science, focusing on practical applications.

- edX – AI for Everyone by Columbia University: Aimed at non-technical learners, this course covers the basics of AI, its implications, and how it is transforming industries.

- Udacity – AI for Business Leaders Nanodegree: This program specifically addresses how to implement AI strategies in business, making it ideal for managers and executives.

2. Books and Publications

- "Artificial Intelligence: A Guide to Intelligent Systems" by Michael Negnevitsky: A comprehensive book that breaks down AI concepts and applications in a format accessible to non-experts.

- "Prediction Machines: The Simple Economics of Artificial Intelligence" by Ajay Agrawal, Joshua Gans, and Avi Goldfarb: This book explores the economic implications of AI and how it changes the cost structure of decision-making.

- "Human + Machine: Reimagining Work in the Age of AI" by Paul R. Daugherty and H. James Wilson: Offers insights into how AI augments human capabilities and transforms business operations.

3. Websites and News Portals

- MIT Technology Review – AI Section: Provides in-depth articles, analyses, and news on AI trends and breakthroughs.

- OpenAI Blog: Regularly updated with technical advancements, research highlights, and discussions on the ethics and future of AI.

- AI Trends: A leading online publication that covers the latest trends, reports, and case studies in artificial intelligence.

4. Podcasts and Videos

- "AI Alignment Podcast": Focuses on the ethical and strategic implications of AI, featuring conversations with leading experts and practitioners.

- "The TWIML AI Podcast (This Week in Machine Learning & AI)": A popular podcast that covers technical and strategic discussions, interviews with AI researchers, and industry case studies.

- "Lex Fridman Podcast": Often features long-form interviews with AI pioneers, scientists, and thinkers, diving deep into the philosophical, technical, and societal aspects of AI.

5. Industry Conferences and Workshops

- NeurIPS (Conference on Neural Information Processing Systems): One of the premier AI conferences, featuring cutting-edge research and workshops that showcase the future of AI technologies.

- AI Summit: Targets business leaders and decision-makers, discussing AI's role in industry transformation and providing networking opportunities with experts.

- TechCrunch Disrupt: While not exclusively focused on AI, this conference is known for presenting innovations that often highlight new AI tools and startups.

6. Professional Networks and Communities

- LinkedIn AI Groups: Numerous groups focus on AI discussions, networking, and sharing insights, such as Artificial Intelligence & Machine Learning and AI Enthusiasts.

- Kaggle: A platform where professionals and enthusiasts collaborate on data science and machine learning projects. It offers tutorials, datasets, and competitions that serve as practical learning experiences.

- Medium AI Publications: Towards Data Science and The Gradient are excellent for exploring in-depth articles, opinion pieces, and practical AI guides written by industry professionals.

7. Government and Regulatory Resources

- OECD AI Policy Observatory: Provides data, analysis, and expert commentary on AI policies and regulations worldwide.

- European Union's AI Watch: Offers insights into how AI is being implemented across member states and tracks policy development in areas like ethical AI.

- U.S. National Artificial Intelligence Initiative Office: A central resource for understanding the federal government's approach to AI, including its strategies, funding opportunities, and partnerships.

END

www.ingramcontent.com/pod-product-compliance
Lightning Source LLC
Chambersburg PA
CBHW070126230526
45472CB00004B/1436